Off the Beat

Off the Beat

My Life as a Brown, Muslim Woman in the Met

**NUSRIT MEHTAB WITH
ANNA WHARTON**

torva

TRANSWORLD PUBLISHERS
Penguin Random House, One Embassy Gardens,
8 Viaduct Gardens, London SW11 7BW
www.penguin.co.uk

Transworld is part of the Penguin Random House group of companies
whose addresses can be found at global.penguinrandomhouse.com

First published in Great Britain in 2024 by Torva
an imprint of Transworld Publishers

Copyright © Nusrit Mehtab 2024

Nusrit Mehtab has asserted her right under the Copyright,
Designs and Patents Act 1988 to be identified as the author of this work.

Every effort has been made to obtain the necessary permissions with
reference to copyright material, both illustrative and quoted. We apologize
for any omissions in this respect and will be pleased to make the
appropriate acknowledgements in any future edition.

As of the time of initial publication, the URLs displayed in this book link
or refer to existing websites on the internet. Transworld Publishers is not
responsible for, and should not be deemed to endorse or recommend,
any website other than its own or any content available on the internet
(including without limitation at any website, blog page, information page)
that is not created by Transworld Publishers.

A CIP catalogue record for this book
is available from the British Library.

ISBN 9781911709459

Typeset in 12/14.5 pt Bembo Book MT Pro by Jouve (UK), Milton Keynes
Printed and bound in Great Britain by Clays Ltd, Elcograf S.p.A.

The authorized representative in the EEA is Penguin Random House Ireland,
Morrison Chambers, 32 Nassau Street, Dublin D02 YH68.

Penguin Random House is committed to a sustainable
future for our business, our readers and our planet. This book
is made from Forest Stewardship Council® certified paper.

For my mum. Her life was a blessing and her memory is a treasure. She continues to inspire me.

Contents

	Prologue	1
1	Hendon	7
2	Leman Street	31
3	Arbour Square	58
4	Charing Cross	79
5	Islington	104
6	Heathrow Airport	130
7	Scotland Yard	144
8	Lambeth Road	174
9	Wood Green	208
10	New Scotland Yard	240
11	The Outside World	253
	Acknowledgements	275

It is not our job as the public to keep ourselves safe from the police. It is the police's job to keep us safe as the public.
— Baroness Casey of Blackstock,
Baroness Casey Review, 2023

In the face of oppression I choose to stand with courage and uphold the banner of justice.
— Imam Hussain

Prologue

It was just before 4.30 a.m. on a chilly morning in early March and my car was weaving through the dark London streets. Most of the roads and buildings were still cast in shadows, though an inky blue sky was beginning to break through between the tall city buildings.

At my window, landmarks flashed by, though not the ones that tourists might recognize. These were the landmarks of my life, more specifically my policing life: an East End pub where I was thrown to the floor in a fight; Westbourne Road, Paddington, where I posed as a decoy to pick up kerb-crawlers; stations where I boarded trains in a niqab for undercover work in serious organized crime and counter terrorism.

Jigsaw pieces of a thirty-year career on the frontline of London's Metropolitan Police.

I was, by now, used to these early mornings: shift work had been the hallmark of my life during my rise through the ranks from PC to superintendent. It hadn't always been a steady climb, though I will come to that. But these days I was more familiar with pre-dawn starts in my roles as a commentator on breakfast television, and as a lecturer to police recruits at the University of East London.

That particular March morning I was being driven to the old BBC Television Centre in White City where *Good Morning Britain* transmits to the nation. In thirty minutes' time I would be in make-up, and an hour or so after that I'd be mic'd up and ready to speak to more than half a million viewers across the country.

As we joined the A40, my driver turned up the radio just in time for the morning's news headlines. 'A new report has revealed that over ninety-nine per cent of police accused of violence against women and girls have kept their jobs,' the newsreader said. 'According to the report by the National Police Chiefs Council more than one thousand five hundred officers and staff have been accused of offences including sexual misconduct over a six-month period . . .'

I sighed. Not because this was news to me, but because so little had changed since I'd entered the force in the late eighties. Some of us have always known this, some of us have felt it personally, but what all of us have in common is that none of us had been heard, and this was the result. No change, a force in ruins, and nothing more than denial from the very top.

On arrival at the studios, I was ushered through the long, winding corridors of Television Centre. After make-up, I was led through to the studio itself. An on-air sign flashed red – an instruction for hushed voices – as we stepped over the camera wires that snaked across the floor. From the side of the set I watched as the presenters, Susanna Reid and Ed Balls, read from the autocue. The Met Police were top of the news agenda, as they had been on many mornings for much of the last couple of years.

As I stood there, my mind went spinning back to my childhood growing up in east London. In my experience, the Met Police had never done anything for the Pakistani community, or any black or Asian community. What these white newsreaders were learning now, we had lived our entire lives. If flats on the council estate where we lived were burgled, we simply turned our furniture back up the right way and got on with it. If skinheads arrived en masse to pick fights in our streets, it was our older brothers who held back the tide of their hatred, never the police. We had simply never thought to call them because we knew their service was not for the likes of us. And as I stood on the side of that *GMB* set, waiting for the ad break during which I would be ushered into my seat, I wondered how the Met Police could possibly be respected now by anyone, of any skin colour.

The truth was that I had joined the police to make a difference from the inside, and when times were tough, when the institution threatened to break me, when I experienced racism and sexism, I stayed because I knew I wasn't the problem. I asked myself why racists and misogynists should keep their jobs while I made myself unemployed. I stayed for all the people who had ever experienced racism, misogyny and homophobia and those who had been victims of bullying. I feared that once I left there would be one less voice speaking out for minorities. But now, if the Met were closing ranks, if they were failing to acknowledge the scale of the problem, it was only by talking about my experiences that I could make a difference. As someone who had been on the inside, I needed to suggest what I felt the force could do to change for the better. Because I believed – I *still* believe even as I write this – that the Metropolitan Police can be a force for good, a force for everyone.

A producer led me on to the set and I shook hands with Susanna and Ed. I sat down in my seat and settled myself in, in time for the cameras to cut back to the presenters after the ad break.

Susanna introduced the topic of the day, the new report stating that less than 1 per cent of police officers and staff accused of abusing women and girls had been sacked. Why? she asked me.

'It's the misconduct process that is not fit for purpose,' I told them both. I had seen it over and over with my own eyes throughout my career. 'So those systems and processes have to be changed. It's great that we've got this data, police chiefs have acknowledged it, the College of Policing has acknowledged it, but what I'd like to see is the chief constable and the Commissioner of Police taking it on board and saying, "Yes, we have a problem, policing is in crisis."'

Because policing *is* in crisis. That's what it comes down to, and there are no two ways about it, there needs to be a shift.

'The scale of cultural change here is absolutely enormous,' Ed Balls said.

And it is, but it is my firm belief that it's not insurmountable.

On live television time moves fast and within minutes our discussion was drawing to a close. But as Ed went to move on, Susanna interrupted him. She read slowly from her notes: 'The force's most senior female ethnic minority officer . . . you would have thought that the force would try harder to keep you, but you had to go.'

For a split second I was caught off guard because, yes, you would have thought so.

'Unfortunately I'm not the only one,' I told Susanna. 'There are a number of us, and it just shows that this problem isn't something that's arrived today, it's been here a long time.'

To this day I think about all the reasons why I couldn't bring myself to stay in a force that time and time again has been found to be institutionally racist, sexist, homophobic and ableist. One that simply refuses to listen. The latest report to find this – the *Baroness Casey Review* – would be published just two weeks after that very interview, and I'd find myself sat on that morning sofa yet again, talking about what needed to change, all the while knowing the Met would ignore it, just like they had everything else.

So, if you can't change a system from the inside, you have no option but to try and change it from the outside. That starts with telling my own story as a brown Muslim woman in the Met.

1

Hendon

Hendon Police College is a formidable building. A bronze statue greets all new arrivals — Sir Robert Peel, the founder of the police service we know today and the reason officers are nicknamed 'bobbies'. He stands before a post-modernist entrance, Peel House, a concrete monolith seemingly held up by four gigantic cone-shaped feet, the very structure of it a monument to the strength and power of the service itself. Behind Peel House is a seventies office building surrounded by tower blocks where new recruits are housed while they complete what was then a gruelling eighteen-week training course. The same course I was there to apply for on that autumn day in 1987.

I could see then that Hendon was a place that would strike a sense of pride, respect, even foreboding into the hearts of many on arrival, perhaps all three. As I stood there, taking it all in, a group of young white men in police uniform came out of the main building and turned left towards the campus. I imagined them as little boys in awe of their local 'bobby', growing up with that uniform in their mind's eye. To them, I thought, this must be a childhood dream finally realized.

That had never been my experience growing up. The honest truth was that I hadn't wanted to join the police, I actually wanted to be an air hostess. That's what I told the careers adviser at university.

'Why do you want to be an air hostess?' she asked, taking a drag on her cigarette.

I paused for a moment, imagining the glamour of working on airlines, the smart uniform, the impeccably turned-out hostesses themselves, the chance to see the world. The careers adviser looked me up and down as if reading my thoughts.

'Stop wasting your time,' she said, holding the cigarette between her lips and reaching for a leaflet from a pile next to her, 'you're too short and too big to be an air hostess.'

I shifted inside my size 14 jeans.

'Anyway, why would you want to be a waitress in the sky?'

She stuck the leaflet she'd reached for in my hand.

'The police are recruiting,' she said, 'go and do something worthwhile.'

And with that she stubbed out her cigarette and I got up from my chair. I was devastated that she had dismissed my dreams, but that wasn't unusual for a woman of colour to experience. I got up, the leaflet in my hand, and left her office.

My heart wasn't set on joining the Metropolitan Police

as I filled in the form, up in the bedroom I shared with my sister. I knew that the police service was not for people like me – a girl of Pakistani origin who had arrived in this country as a toddler, and who started school with no grasp of the English language. My mum spoke to us only in Urdu or Punjabi. I'd never seen a person with brown skin in a police uniform, let alone a female police officer.

So why did I apply? As a proud Londoner, as an East Ender, I wanted to make things better for people like me – those ignored by the police force who were supposed to keep us safe. Plus, I had grown up listening to stories of my uncle who had been a policeman back in Pakistan. I knew that this job could make a difference.

I didn't tell my mum or my siblings, just in case it didn't go anywhere. I only told Nina Chaudhary, my best friend from secondary school, who was supportive even though she couldn't really understand my sudden interest in the police force. I knew that the interview at Hendon involved a fitness test so I began to do some training down at the local track and pool, limping round at a snail's pace, out of breath and wheezing from the exertion, but determined to improve my time, day after day, week after week. A couple of months later I was running round the entire 400-metre track and had forgotten all about being an air hostess. Getting fit alone had given me a reason to want the police to accept me.

I checked in that morning at Hendon and was interviewed by three white middle-aged men in uniform who asked me why I wanted to be a police officer. I stumbled on my words as I answered their questions. I wondered how many new recruits like me they had interviewed, how many people with my skin colour, how many females. All the recruits I'd seen walking around Hendon were white men.

After my interview, it was time for the physical. At the gymnasium we were put through our paces: sprints, press-ups, jumping jacks, and then the track for the run that I had worked so hard for. I surprised myself with how fit I had become and was relieved and thrilled when I ran faster than some of the other recruits.

Next, we were sent to see the doctor for the medical. The female recruits – of which there seemed to be just a handful among the group – had been told they would need to wear a bra and knickers for the medical examination. I had ignored that instruction, not seeing the relevance, and wore an all-in-one leotard and leggings under my T-shirt and jeans. I sat in the waiting room anxiously, but before long the doctor's secretary called my name and took me into the changing room, telling me to take off my clothes and go into the little room in my underwear. I walked through in my leotard and leggings to see an old white-haired man sitting behind a solid oak desk.

I stood in front of him as he looked down at his notes. He asked me some questions without looking up: height, weight, did I smoke, did I drink?

'Right, take your top off and touch your toes,' he said.

'No,' I said firmly, the shock apparent in my voice.

He looked up from his notes for the first time and opened his mouth to say something, but perhaps it was the look of defiance on my face that stole the words from him. I stood there, he sat there. I could see he didn't quite know what to say. It was clear he wasn't used to women refusing his orders. In that particular moment I wasn't trying to find the logic in why female recruits needed to remove their bras, I was just affronted at being asked to do so. And he could see that. After an awkward few moments he dismissed me, writing something in his notes. I hurried out of the room.

Outside, another woman was waiting to be called. As I left, the nurse was showing her to the changing room and asking her to strip to her bra and knickers.

It seemed that my refusal to strip off had not stood in my way of being recruited, because a few weeks later a letter arrived at our Walthamstow home. I opened it with shaking hands, wondering if I'd passed or failed. I was so delighted to read I had been accepted by the Metropolitan Police, that I had achieved what I had set out to do. But that excitement was quickly replaced with a feeling of dread at having to then go and tell Mum.

I read the letter to her in our kitchen. She had never properly learnt English, either to speak it or to read it, so me and my siblings had spent our childhoods reading out to her official letters and school reports.

'What are you doing, *pagal kuri*?' she said – meaning 'crazy girl' in Punjabi. 'You really want to do this?'

This was the first time that I had told her of my plans and she was surprised to put it mildly, not least because the eighteen-week residential course meant that I would be leaving home for the first time. I could see on her face that she was concerned about my decision, but she kept the specifics of those doubts to herself.

'Well, if you're going to do this,' Mum said, adjusting her headscarf and going back to chopping onions and garlic, 'don't come back and complain about it, because you will.'

I'll always remember that moment because I never did go back and complain. Not once, not in all the years that followed, through all the ups and downs of my thirty-year career. It was tough, sometimes unbearably so, but I never brought my troubles back to our kitchen table. That day, holding that letter, marked the start of a new chapter for me, a new challenge – though I perhaps didn't realize then just how challenging it would be.

Why the hesitation from my family? Why did they not hold the Metropolitan Police in the same esteem that others might? To answer that question, you would need to know what was happening in London at that time. I arrived at Hendon in the late eighties, the decade that saw the Brixton Riots and the *Scarman Report* (which found the Metropolitan Police Service to be institutionally racist), and just a few years before Stephen Lawrence would be murdered while standing at a bus stop in south London.

It was an age of racism. It was the age of the skinheads, of the National Front who would march on my area in Walthamstow. We didn't see them, Mum saw to that, but as I said, it was my brothers and other Asian and black boys who would hold back their marches on our streets. The police never came to our aid when we called, and the odd time they did attend a domestic incident our mothers quickly shooed us back into our flats. They knew how easy it was to end up on the wrong side of an officer. Doors would slam closed, while everyone watched from behind the safety of their net curtains.

As children we quickly learnt that the police might be there to serve, but not people with our skin colour.

Officers were as white as the public they protected. They looked angry, aggressive. To me as a child, they looked like the skinheads that thundered down our streets.

When the New Cross house fire happened in 1981, thirteen young black lives were lost. Tensions spilled on to the streets and violent clashes took place between police and the black community just the other side of the river from where we sat watching on our TV set. I saw the anger emanating from both sides in that grainy black and white TV news footage. I had experienced it first-hand when I was three or four years old, walking home from the shops one Saturday afternoon with my mum and my sister. Her arms were heavy with bags of fruit and vegetables when we saw them from the end of the road – a gang of skinheads coming straight at us.

Mum's hand instantly gripped tighter around mine. She pushed us into a nearby phone box, pulling the door closed behind us. I remember her bloodless fingertips holding the half-moon-shaped handle with all her strength and I tried to grip it too, even though I could barely reach it, trying to help her, terrified as the men on the other side fought to pull the door open. Through the small oblong windows I saw their faces, shoved up against the glass – wild eyes, sharp teeth, shaved heads.

Mum ordered us in Punjabi to bury our faces in her clothes. But I could still hear them.

'Paki!' they spat. 'Go home!'

London was our home.

They kicked at the phone box with steel-capped boots and roared vicious insults. People walked by but no one stopped them.

How long was it before they'd finished having their

fun? A minute, two, five? Who knows. We emerged from the phone box shaking and crying. No one asked if we were OK.

Mum held our hands tight as we hurried home, and she put us to bed that night with beautiful stories so we wouldn't have nightmares – stories of her village back in Pakistan, of our grandfather's house and all the wonderful colours of its rooms. She told us how my grandfather was a respected man, how all the villagers sought counsel from him, how our family home was the centre of village life, how ladies would arrive each morning to sell twinkling bangles or silk scarves, or brought chapattis as gifts for her family, and mango, and dried fruits that glittered like coloured jewels, 'Like nothing you have ever tasted before,' she said.

This experience was one of an endless string of racial attacks that were ubiquitous for people like us. This was the London we knew. No wonder, then, that we didn't regard the police as the paragons of protection that they were to everyone else. They simply didn't view us as their responsibility.

Within months, I was standing outside Hendon Police College again, holding tight on to a bag full of clothes, and heavy with apprehension. For the next eighteen weeks this north London metropolis was to be my home. My cohort was shown around the campus, though it felt daunting, more like an army base. Two classes marched past us in unison, their captain calling out orders as they stopped and stood to attention. This was not what I had expected.

We were divided into two classes, each consisting of

around twenty new recruits. I glanced around at my fellow students, all in deep conversation with one another, while I watched on in silence. They all seemed eager to learn, but, inevitably, what most of them had in common was the fact that they were all white men. We were told that our intake had the largest number of non-white recruits the Met had ever had, but we still only made up a handful in a sea of white. In my class there were three of us: myself, a dual-heritage girl and an Armenian guy. In the other class were a couple of girls who looked as though they might be from a Mediterranean background and one black guy.

The dual-heritage girl in my class was Cherry Farley, and our eyes locked – we had clearly been making the same assessment of the cohort. We smiled at each other and I felt relief then, that there would be someone there I could connect with. Cherry and I were sharing a dorm in one of the giant tower blocks. The dormitories were divided into men and women and within each one was a communal kitchen and bathroom, then four or five individual bedrooms, each with a single bed. Cherry and I would end up spending a lot of time in each other's rooms every evening, revising for our assessments, ironing our shirts or shining our shoes for inspection the following morning. The other recruits preferred the campus bar, but Cherry and I noticed that we were never invited to join them.

Cherry became my confidante. She was a real gentle soul, an east London girl like me, though not someone you might consider a typical police officer. She was caring, grounded, and didn't push herself to the front. She observed everything and had a quiet confidence about her. Both of us felt we didn't belong there, which is perhaps why we clicked instantly. I asked her if she'd also been requested to take off her bra at the strange medical exam upon entry.

She said she had. 'I didn't think at the time to refuse to do it,' she said, sadly.

There was an immediate camaraderie among the other recruits, based mostly around their drinking culture, so Cherry and I and some of the BAME men on the course were instantly identifiable as 'the outsiders'. And it wasn't just the new recruits propping up the bar: the instructors drank with them, as well as the recruits who were further down the line on their training course and who would gladly give out the answers to various assessments after a few drinks. Cherry and I realized early on that we either needed to drink to get ahead, or do what people of colour have always done and work twice as hard as our white counterparts. We chose the latter.

This 'othering' we experienced extended to the canteens too. At lunchtime the other recruits sat together, leaving Cherry and me and a couple of the other people of colour to sit separately with our food.

Even aside from the social hierarchies at Hendon, the course itself was tough. We were up early each day for classes, even earlier when we were parading. Parade happened come rain or shine, and when someone in our line got it wrong, our instructors ordered us to get up early and practise before class the following morning. We had never marched before, and we weren't taught how to do it, so you could often find us out on the main concourse at five o'clock in the morning or late at night marching up and down to get it right. Cherry and I would always look at each other with a sly smile or roll our eyes during practice, though if any of the inspectors caught us we'd get told off like school girls. It felt so alien for us to be marching as if we were army recruits, but some of the men seemed to love it and took it so seriously, that and shining their shoes every evening. They behaved as if they were soldiers in the British Army.

It was for this reason that most cohort groups chose a peer with military experience as class captain so they could show them how to march. It surprised me just how much emphasis was put on military-style parades, and uniform inspections, which I came to dread, but looking back I think what they were trying to establish was a sense of the discipline and hierarchy that ran through the Metropolitan Police. A hierarchy that I would climb myself over the next three decades.

But studying until late at night and then parading in pouring rain not long after dawn had broken was not something that I relished. I would return home to east London each weekend having packed my bag for what I insisted was the last time, and telling Nina that I wasn't going back for the following week.

'You don't have to do this, Nusrit,' Nina insisted, 'but if anybody can, it's you. So go back out there and smash it – you're not a quitter.'

She was right, Nina always was, and every Sunday evening I would emerge out of the Hendon Central Underground Station with a holdall full of freshly ironed clothes for the week ahead, ready to do it all again.

I guess I had decided to approach Hendon as I had everything else in my life. I knew because I was a woman, because of the colour of my skin, that people didn't expect me to last. I was determined to prove the doubters wrong, to keep showing up, that no one should underestimate me. It was up to me to decide where I belonged and where I didn't.

Our course took place over the summer, so Monday to Friday was spent in classrooms where the same hot air circulated and made our heads feel heavy. In those stuffy classrooms we learnt various parts of policing: how to stop and search; what grounds you need to do so; traffic offences; drink driving laws; violent offences; self-defence; and, above all, how to complete paperwork – reams of paperwork. Each module was followed by an assessment, and Cherry and I spent night after night in our rooms pouring over our books while we waxed our arms and legs and gossiped about our instructors.

There was a distinction at Hendon between the more experienced recruits and the newbies who had to wear their own clothes for the first two weeks. We were all tired of sticking out like sore thumbs and so there was a buzz about the place the day we were told we were getting our uniforms.

It meant, however, a new layer of anxiety when it came to parades. Every item of our uniform would have to be perfect, from our hats to the tips of our shoes, which we were shown how to buff to a shine. We would be inspected every morning. Cherry and I would stand in our dorm using masking tape to tease any bits of fluff from each other's tunics before parade.

To receive this hallowed uniform, we were sent to a lady in a Portakabin on site who must have seen every shape and size before. Around her neck hung a tape measure which she wielded deftly, measuring students up in seconds and handing them a pile of uniform that would inevitably fit perfectly. For a one-woman band she ran an efficient production line, a conveyor belt of recruits that fell off the other end as fully equipped officers. She filled each set of outstretched arms with three of each item: shirts, ties, trousers and helmets for the men, hats, blouses, skirts and handbags for the women plus a stocking allowance with advice to buy the same denier stockings to 'keep things uniform'. We had to buy our own shoes; an advert in the police magazine told us where to go to get them. The men wore Doc Martens, which did little to dissuade me from my childhood belief that policemen were just skinheads in uniform.

Finally it was my turn at the front of the queue.

'Size?' the lady barked, reaching round to the shelf of skirts, her hand hovering, waiting for my answer.

'Oh, I don't wear skirts,' I said, quietly.

She pretended that she hadn't heard me. 'Size?' she said again.

'I don't wear skirts,' I tried again, a little louder.

She turned around, looked me up and down to assess my size, and pulled a selection from the shelves behind her.

'Here are your three skirts,' she said, putting them into my arms.

'But I don't wear skirts.'

'Well, I haven't got anything else,' she said, 'you'll just have to wear tights with them.'

She measured my neck size for shirts and my head for a hat, ignoring my protestations.

I felt the eyes of everyone else in the queue on me, heard the impatient sighs, felt the restlessness of those behind me. I was too embarrassed to look back.

'Hurry up,' someone shouted.

'But I don't have anything to wear,' I said.

'Just take the skirts anyway,' the lady said, and then looked behind me. 'Next!'

I left the skirts on her counter and carried my uniform, bar the bottom half, out of the cabin, almost tripping over because I was carrying so much.

When I joined the Met I hadn't thought that women might not be allowed to wear trousers. In the outside world, women all around me wore them, it was perfectly normal, so why not the police in the late 1980s? It wasn't that I merely disliked skirts. I was raised a Muslim, and in my community we chose to wear trousers for modesty reasons. It would never even have occurred to me to wear a skirt.

Back in class, I went to speak to my instructor.

'I haven't got all of my uniform,' I told him, explaining to him that I didn't wear skirts, not today, not yesterday, not ever. 'It's not part of my culture,' I explained. 'We wear trousers instead.'

He looked shocked at my suggestion that I should wear trousers. 'Women don't wear trousers here,' he said.

'Well, I don't wear skirts.'

For me there just wasn't a choice. It wasn't a case of just going along with the status quo.

'Leave it with me,' my tutor said with a sigh that let me know I was making things difficult for him – and likely for myself.

Back in our student digs, all my peers were busy trying on their uniform, checking themselves out in the mirror excitedly, complimenting each other on the fit. It was impossible not to feel isolated; I stood out more than I already felt I did. I tied my hair in a bun and tried on my hat along with Cherry and then we both examined ourselves in the mirror.

'I understand if it's against your principles,' Cherry said while brushing down her own uniform in the mirror. 'I wish I could ask for trousers in solidarity, they'd be much more comfortable. How are you supposed to chase someone in a skirt anyway?'

That hadn't been my point of course, but it was a good one. Why did the police insist women wear skirts and stockings when it didn't seem practical?

The following morning I had no choice but to turn up on parade in my own clothes.

'Why aren't you in uniform?' people asked as we marched.

I felt that familiar sting of humiliation and embarrassment. I had to explain myself over and over again. I saw how my classmates wrinkled their brows, unable to understand.

'Couldn't you just wear a skirt?' one after another said.

It was obvious they thought I was being difficult, and nobody wants to be associated with a problem. I'd never sat with them during breaks in the canteen, but somehow I noticed that they now kept their distance even more than before. I didn't hear anything from the tutors. Perhaps they felt if they left me long enough I'd fall into line like everyone else. I saw other brown girls, one or two Indian girls, in skirts – perhaps their religion allowed it, perhaps they had decided not to speak up. But that wasn't me.

I saw the looks the other students gave me. For them there was no problem, no issue, they were used to things being a certain way, they never thought to question it, nor did they need to. The system worked for them, and anyone who asked for that system to work differently was obviously a problem. The Met might have been ready to allow more diversity on to its roll call, but they hadn't anticipated having to adapt for us. I knew that they were thinking I was expecting special treatment, but they needed to see it was the system itself that refused to bend and shape to its changing demographic.

The following day the inspector appeared on parade. He was your stereotypical military man: straight back, pace stick tucked firmly under his arm. I didn't like this inspector, nor many of the instructors. I had heard the way some of them spoke about the other recruits. One once called our Armenian friend, Basil, a 'carpet trader' and a 'sheep herder'.

'He shouldn't be saying that to you,' Cherry and I had told him after class.

'I know, but what can I do?' he said.

Another time a sergeant told Cherry he expected more from her in physical exercise, the racist stereotype being that a tall black woman is meant to excel at sports.

'Miss Mehtab,' the inspector said in a stern voice making a point of pronouncing every syllable of my name to emphasize its strangeness to him, 'why are you not in your uniform?'

I felt the whole parade's eyes on me as the inspector singled me out.

'I don't have a uniform, sir.'

One of the other tutors stepped forward and whispered something in his ear. He moved on. I spent the rest of the day expecting to be called into the inspector's office and screamed at, but it never happened.

Finally, weeks after everyone else got their uniform, one of the instructors called me into the staff room.

'You're going to get trousers,' he said, not looking up from his desk.

Apparently it had taken so long because the uniform change had had to be approved at the highest level by an assistant commissioner in consultation with the Met's Diversity Unit. It would be years until the uniform policy changed and other women would be issued trousers. I was just thrilled that I would no longer stand out as different, that I could blend in with the other recruits.

The instructor dismissed me to the uniform hut to go and collect them.

'There are no women's trousers,' the lady behind the counter said, handing me three pairs of men's trousers. I questioned why, if I was getting men's trousers, I'd had to wait weeks. She didn't reply and pulled the shutter down.

'I look like Charlie Chaplin,' I groaned to Cherry as I tried on my uniform for the first time. The trousers swamped my 5ft 4in frame, the hems gobbling up my feet.

'You're not even allowed to adjust them,' she said, shaking her head.

She was right. All uniform remained the property of the Met Police, so we weren't allowed to tamper with it or get anything tailored to fit.

Perhaps the instructors hoped that the humiliation of wearing those ill-fitting trousers might force me into giving up on my resolve not to wear skirts. But they didn't know me very well. Each day I appeared on parade, I had buffed my shoes until they shone, as instructed, except no one could see them under my trousers. I marched in all weathers like that until the hems were scuffed and dirty. But at least I hadn't yielded. After a few weeks of this I took my trousers home and got them re-hemmed, and none of the instructors noticed.

The Met might have been ready to diversify their recruits in name, but not in reality. There were no policies in place for adapting workplaces or uniforms for those from different cultural backgrounds. These recruits were simply expected to fit in and to show the same respect to the institution as their white counterparts. When they didn't, the Met were quite happy for them to be 'othered'. It's strange to think about it now: I always thought I wasn't ready for the Met, when in reality it was the Met that weren't ready for me.

I faced a similar issue at swimming practice. All the men turned up to the pool in shorts, all the women in swimsuits. Everyone, including the swimming tutors, my class instructors and even the sergeant, stood at the side of the pool expectantly, their hands behind their backs, wondering what I was going to come out in. I finally found the courage and emerged from the changing room in a full-length leotard and leggings with my swimming costume on over the top – an idea Nina had suggested. It was very daunting to come out and see them all waiting for me.

'We were wondering if you would come out,' someone whispered as I took my place in line.

During sports practice I refused to wear a short PE skirt and instead wore tracksuit bottoms. Cherry was so tall, she too felt uncomfortable in the short PE skirts and decided to wear knee-length cycling shorts, but the instructors were furious and ordered her to take them off.

Over the last thirty years, the Met Police have done a lot to improve the number of recruits that come from diverse backgrounds, but they still have a long way to go. The majority of London's population is not from a white British background. One in five residents do not even speak English as their first language, yet in contrast, 82 per cent of Met police officers are white and 71 per cent of them are male. The majority of officers do not even live in the city they patrol, and so the Met doesn't actually represent the people that it serves.

Public trust in the Met has been falling for many years, from a high of 89 per cent in 2016 to a low of 66 per cent in March 2022, made worse by the rooting out of rogue officers after the murder of Sarah Everard by serving Metropolitan Police officer Wayne Couzens in 2021. People from black and mixed ethnic groups have an even lower trust in the force, scoring between 10 and 20 per cent lower than average, and surveys undertaken for Baroness Casey's review published in the wake of Sarah Everard's murder revealed that, when asked, two in five Londoners think the Met's external reputation is poor, and black Londoners are even more likely to agree. But is that any wonder when the demographic of the force that is meant to serve them is so far from that of London itself? We had two reports before Baroness Casey's review, the *Scarman Report* in 1981 and the *Macpherson Report* in 1999, that found the Metropolitan Police Service to be institutionally racist, and still the Met rejects that label.

'Since publication of the Macpherson report in 1999,' wrote Baroness Casey in her review, 'the Met has remained largely white and largely male. If recruitment continues on its current trajectory, it will take at least another thirty years, until 2053, to reach gender balance. It will take even longer, until 2061, to reach 46% Black, Asian and ethnic minority representation – what is needed to be representative of London today, let alone the even more diverse city it will be in nearly 40 years' time.'

The problem is, of course, that with its current reputation and repeated denials from the Met chiefs, the service is not managing to attract the very people it needs to meet this target. The delivery date for the Uplift Programme, a government drive to recruit an extra 20,000 police officers in England and Wales, was March 2023: the Met has missed its own target of recruiting 40 per cent of its new recruits from ethnic backgrounds and therefore lost £3.8 million of its funding. The current Commissioner of Police Sir Mark Rowley says that for 2024 the Met will be 6,000 officers short.

That target was agreed after London's mayor, Sadiq Khan, ordered new research that found that black people in the capital were six times more likely than white people to be stopped while driving. Official figures showed that black people are disproportionately hit by key police powers, tactics and use of force. Given that backdrop, why would people from BAME backgrounds be attracted to the police? When people of colour do join the organization, they are not long lasting. Around 62 per cent of BAME people leave within two years. It's no wonder. Even as a naive twenty-one-year-old recruit I saw just how hostile an environment it was.

Baroness Casey's review concluded that while the Met had conducted exercises to gather facts on the diverse communities it represents, it still did not understand them and 'does not translate these into plans or use them to recalibrate the services it delivers'. She wrote: 'While the Met has aspirations to engage with London's communities, it does not do enough to make its workforce look like and represent the make-up of the community it polices, undermining both trust and confidence, and effectiveness.'

A little like the drive when I joined to recruit a more diverse range of officers, there was no understanding then, and seemingly no understanding now, of people from those communities. That's why they didn't appreciate my insistence that I must wear trousers, that request alone marking me out for years as a 'troublemaker' and someone who wanted 'special treatment'. It immediately 'othered' me among my cohort, but that wasn't my fault. It was the Met's, because they did not understand people from my community, they just wanted us in the force as a 'token' of their diversity.

For me, these targets the organizations set are just piecemeal. They make great headlines, but where is the work they are doing to back it up? Macpherson gave them a similar target back in the late nineties, but the Met didn't make that then and I don't think they can make it now. Especially not when they refuse to accept – despite report after report, allegation after allegation, anecdote after anecdote – that they are a racist organization. That admission alone would signify to black and Asian communities that they acknowledge the problem, and then they can start to address it. Just admitting that would build trust in those communities. But the Met tend to see this as a sign of weakness rather than strength. I think back to when I cowered in the phone box with my mother and sister, never once considering to contact the police, and wonder what a difference it would've made to have a police force that represented us.

The second thing the Met need to do is get behind the London Police Race Action Plan and show a real commitment to tackling racism by resourcing it fully with full-time staff, not just volunteers. There needs to be an external independent body of investigators that deals with allegations of discrimination and sexual misconduct if we want racial justice. The Met have proved they are unfit to do this. This body can't be the Independent Office for Police Conduct (IOPC) because there is an enduring and inevitable problem with the patriarchy and old boys' network. The police watchdog is ineffective.

The Met need to show they are passionate about promoting police accountability and community safety. The Met need to focus on the career paths of BAME officers; new recruits need to see people like them at the upper echelons of policing. There is a lot of truth in the saying 'You cannot be what you cannot see'.

I believe that the new commissioner needs to call for a Royal Commission. It would carry more weight than these external reviews, because even the bodies who regulate the police say they are powerless. In June 2023, Andy Cooke, the head of His Majesty's Inspectorate of Constabulary and Fire & Rescue Services (HMICFRS), demanded sweeping new powers to compel police forces to act in what he described as 'the worst crisis in law and order in living memory'. 'Public trust in the police is hanging by a thread,' he said, citing the murder of Sarah Everard by Wayne Couzens, and the multiple rape convictions of another Met officer, David Carrick, as cases in point. Cooke urged the government to introduce legislation to make it a legal requirement for police forces to follow directions and recommendations, and said that some public scandals to have come out of the Met in recent years might have been avoidable if those recommendations had been implemented.

In 2021, HMICFRS started the Race and Policing Programme that would inspect police forces for their commitment and contribution towards eliminating discrimination, advancing equality of opportunity, and fostering good relations with black and ethnic minority communities. But without legal powers afforded to them by the government, even the policing inspectorate recognize they will not see any real change, and sadly, neither will new BAME recruits.

Despite the divide in race, we had all built a certain camaraderie by the end of our eighteen weeks at Hendon. We had to, in order to survive the experience. If one of us failed, we all failed. If one of us couldn't march, we all had to practise. If one person hadn't buffed their shoes, none of us passed inspection. While at the start that felt extremely unfair, it made us look out for each other. I wouldn't go so far as to say the white recruits were friendly towards us outsiders, but we all shared a mutual respect.

Towards the end of our course we were sent to a training site in Hounslow, west London, to do public order training. There our instructors staged a riot, which we were expected to contain. It was frightening. We were armed with batons and shields, and in a mock-fight our instructors came running towards us, even throwing firebombs, their faces twisted in anger, and playing sounds over a loudspeaker of a baying mob. It reminded me so much of those skinheads that surrounded the phone box that day. If that was just our instructors pretending, I could not imagine the real thing. We held our line with our shields out in front of us. They were heavy and not meant for small women like me, but I held my own. The day left me exhausted and wondering what I'd got myself into.

In our penultimate week we were assigned the stations we would be posted to. Our instructors pinned our postings up in the main hall and everyone scrambled to see where they were being sent. Cherry and I pushed our way to the front and, amid excited chatter, found our names.

'I'm being posted west,' Cherry said.

'I'm being posted east,' I sighed, disappointed we wouldn't be working together.

I had become used to Hendon by now. With Cherry's and Nina's help I had got through the training and now I was a fully fledged graduate of the police college. On our final day for our passing-out parade I felt proud of everything that I had achieved, that I had lasted the course. I would need to do two years on probation at an actual station before I was fully qualified. But did I feel prepared for real policing? Maybe it wasn't the policing that was going to be the hard part.

2

Leman Street

I was told to report for duty at Leman Street Police Station in Whitechapel a week after graduating in November 1988. A police station has stood on that site since 1830 when a division co-opted a house there. As it grew, they took over two houses just up the road, plus a former warehouse that was fitted with cells and reached via a covered passageway. Little did they know then that during the killing spree of Jack the Ripper that began in 1888 these humble premises would see the launch of one of the biggest inquiries in Metropolitan Police history.

But that day a century later, the building was barely recognizable. This version of the station had been built in the late sixties and comprised six storeys faced with Portland stone, looking more like an office block than a traditional police station. The ground floor accommodated the cells, the interview rooms and the public inquiry office, which is where I presented myself for duty.

We had been pre-warned in Hendon that our first three or four weeks of service would be what is known as 'street duty'. New probationers would be assigned a 'street duty instructor' who would take us out walking the beat – a parent constable if you like. Stations were made up of various departments and response teams were divided into A, B, C and D, and each of those teams would be assigned a shift – early, day, night or overnight. I was to be on nights. Street duty was seen as an integration process to help new recruits get used to the day-to-day formalities of police work and get to know the area they'd be covering. It gave new recruits time to practise duties like stopping cars, or carrying out stop and searches. There were four of us on street duties who'd all come from Hendon together, so it didn't feel too daunting.

My street duty instructor's name was Pete. He was tall and skinny and looked like a boy who'd been stretched into a man, though I would later learn he had been an officer for ten years. He was also a response car driver, though that day we would be on foot. The sergeant told us we would be patrolling in the Commercial Road area.

'Ready?' Pete said, his eyes falling to my trousers. He looked surprised. I guessed it was his first time seeing a female officer in trousers.

Commercial Road is a nearly two-mile stretch of arterial road across the East End. We headed towards it on foot and as we did so Pete gave me an overview of the area. Commercial Road was made up of many Asian shops as it was an area which had always been populated by migrant families: Jewish, Irish, Bengali, you name it, although these days you're more likely to find a hipster there. Long before the smart coffee shops of today there were food wholesalers, off licences, leather shops and fabric factories similar to the one my mum worked in. I tried to concentrate on what Pete was telling me. It felt so different from Hendon, being out on the streets; for one thing we didn't have to march and no one cared how shiny our shoes were. Only as we continued down the road I noticed that many of the shopkeepers were coming out to watch us go by. I caught a couple of them pointing, talking to each other in Urdu. It was obvious that it was us they were staring at. As we passed one group of men standing in the doorway of a shop, one of them asked in Urdu where I was from. I replied that I was from east London.

'Do they usually do this?' I asked Pete.

He glanced over at them, perhaps noticing them for the first time. 'No,' he said. 'I think it's you they've come to see.'

It was at that moment that I caught a glimpse of myself in a shop window and saw what looked like a fully-fledged police officer staring back. It dawned on me what they were coming out to look at: a brown woman in police uniform, something none of them had ever seen before. To those shopkeepers I was now 'one of them' – a police officer, part of an institution that had never done anything for their families. It felt suddenly as if I didn't belong in one world or another, and the enormity of the job hit me for the first time. This wasn't training school any more with its practice scenarios and pretend thugs, this was the real thing – real people, real cars, real streets. And I felt a huge sense of responsibility to get this right for the community. I was now policing people who looked like me.

Pete led the way that day, and started by showing me how to stop cars. He demonstrated for me first, pulling a car over. I wasn't sure why he had chosen that particular car, but he instructed the man driving it to get out and stand on the side of the road. He indicated to me to follow him around the car, where he showed me how to look for problems. He looked at the tyres, then pulled at some of the rubber, which came away in his hands.

'You see that?' he said.

I nodded, unsure of whether he'd just caused the problem he had found.

'That's illegal,' he said.

He instructed me how to write out a ticket for the driver though I felt uneasy doing it, and moments later we walked away, leaving the driver with the dilemma of his now-ruined tyres.

We continued down Commercial Road, Pete showing me the best places to stand to catch cars using the bus lane or running red lights. We stopped more cars, I took more notes, checked licences and radioed number plates into the control room to check for insurance and MOTs. I was suddenly aware of the effect a police uniform had on someone, how it marked you out as different, perhaps even gave you a sense of power. Or at least that's what I noticed in Pete.

Over the next few months I would find the pressure I was under to meet my quota for stop and searches every day was intense. Even today, the new recruits I lecture tell me that they are still under this same pressure during their probation period, and often that pressure overrides the requirement for reasonable grounds. Usually, grounds might be someone behaving in a suspicious way, or recognizing a local criminal who is known to carry knives or drugs. While these guidelines don't specify race, it is well documented that black people are six times more likely to be stopped and searched than white people. It is not that the Met teach recruits to stop black people more often, it is their own unconscious bias, their own psyche, that tells them to stop them. Often, on the rare occasions when I walked with colleagues, I saw how easily they found a reason to stop someone, telling them that they fitted the description of a criminal operating in that area or that they could smell cannabis. It made me uncomfortable to witness how they gravitated towards certain demographics. To them it was just another search ticked off the list, but for the public these experiences can be humiliating and scary. I know that many working officers still do not understand what reasonable grounds are – stopping a black man for wearing a big overcoat in the summer (as a police officer did in Croydon in 2022) is not reasonable. We are supposed to be identifying threats rather than acting on our own biases. Despite this lack of knowledge of the law as it stands, the government has recently extended police powers to stop and search. This sort of behaviour is the kind the police need to work on, but it is impossible if an organization – or a human – won't recognize the unconscious bias there in the first place.

As Pete and I continued our walk he pointed out cafés, where best to go to get a sandwich or a cup of tea.

'Or doughnuts if you're late,' he added.

I must have looked confused.

'And you bring in cream cakes when it's your birthday,' he said, 'those are the rules. Plus the probationers make the tea for the entire parade, so you'll have to find out how everyone takes it.'

It was clear that being the probationer was the lowest rung on the ladder, but the culture was so established that if I wanted to fit in I'd need to be prepared to follow even the oddest of station rules. I know that these hierarchies still exist within police stations. Probationers are pressured to fit in with the way things have always been done and so the culture never moves with the times. To earn their place the lowest ranks serve tea to their fellow officers, the sergeants, the inspectors, the area car drivers (whom I would come to learn are the god-like figures of any team) and even those in the control room.

No amount of training can prepare you for walking into the parade room in uniform for the very first time. This is when you meet your new team – and I would be joining D team. It is the epitome of being thrown in at the deep end. The room I walked into was in the bowels of Leman Street Police Station and was so loud and buzzing with people that none of my new colleagues noticed me walk in. They were all gathered for the beginning of their shift, waiting for the duty sergeant to arrive. Every shift he would call out their numbers, pair them up with a colleague and let them know where they would be patrolling. Though utterly intimidating for a probationer like me, the atmosphere was jovial rather than serious. Colleagues who seemed to know each other well passed around tea, coffee, even doughnuts. There was a teasing, flirting culture that was alien to me compared to the strict background I'd come from.

I went and stood in the corner and watched it all with curiosity and amusement. Observing the room, I saw it was mostly made up of men, with just one or two uniformed women. But what surprised me was that the room was completely white. Even compared to Hendon, this room was noticeably devoid of officers of colour. I was the only brown person there, and yet I appeared to have gone completely unnoticed.

A second later the sergeant walked in, head down, staring at his paperwork, and the room instantly quietened down. He was probably somewhere between forty and fifty with a tiny moustache and a big belly. I noticed as he called out our numbers that he was well spoken, handing out orders efficiently as he divided up an area which stretched from the Tower of London to Brick Lane and Mile End Road.

'347 you're with 252,' he said, 'you'll be in the area car today. 621 you're on foot with 198 . . .'

'269?' The sergeant called out my number. 'How do I say your name?'

'Nusrit,' I replied.

'Oh I can't say that,' he said. 'What's your English name?'

'My name is Nusrit.'

'Nidgit?'

The rest of the team sniggered.

'No, Nusrit. N-U-S-R-I-T. You say it as it's spel—'

'I'll call you Nidgit,' he said, dismissing us.

From then on, my new routine began. Each shift I'd arrive in the parade room and everyone would turn to look at me expectantly. With everyone's eyes on me, I felt really awkward and uncomfortable. I'd go and put the kettle on, clean the cups, and make everyone tea the way I quickly learnt they liked it. Milky, builder's, black, there was even one person who took six sugars! While the tea brewed, I observed the parade room as per usual. I'd learnt from Pete that many of these officers had worked together for years, and just like at Hendon, they too went drinking together after their shifts. It was common to come off a shift in the early hours and go straight to a club they knew would still be serving. One of my main observations was the way the women acted around the men, and how differently they talked about them in our female-only changing room. Out in the parade room the females laughed at their dirty jokes and their banter – especially Bernie, who worked in the control room and had clearly been there decades. She gave as good as she got and they always teased her.

And it wasn't just 'banter'. The men would try and touch the women too. 'Let's see if you're wearing the full kit,' they laughed, trying to feel for the stockings and suspenders beneath their skirts. Sometimes the women let them, other times they batted their hands away playfully.

Everything was done in jest out on the floor, the women cautious not to cause offence, but when it was just the few of us in the women's changing room they let their frustrations show, moaning about what leches they all were and how they hated how they behaved. Perhaps, in their minds, there had been progress – things weren't as bad as they used to be. Bernie told me that the male officers used to initiate female staff by holding them down over the desk, pulling up their skirt and imprinting the office stamp on their buttocks.

'That's awful,' I said.

She laughed. 'At least they don't do that any more.'

Most of the women there just shrugged them off, or they swore along with the men, telling them details of their sex lives when they asked. I noticed that those were the women the men described as 'all right'.

'Why don't you complain?' I asked whenever they moaned after a particularly egregious shift.

'To who?' they laughed. 'The inspector is even worse.'

I knew who they meant. They had nicknamed this inspector 'Handy' because he had a habit of groping the women in full view of the office: slipping an arm around a shoulder and resting his hand on the side of a breast, or his favourite habit of standing in narrow doorways and refusing to move so female officers had to squeeze between him and the door frame, his fat belly pushed up against them.

He tried it on me once.

'Come on then, Nidgit,' he said, waving me through.

I refused. I'd seen him play this trick on countless other girls and would not submit myself to it. We stood for a moment in a stand-off, everyone watching us, wondering what the inspector might do – he clearly wasn't used to being challenged. Finally, he moved, mumbling something about getting back to his office. In some ways I felt sorry for my white colleagues who weren't brave enough to do the same. It was almost that they maintained the status quo simply because they were too scared to say no.

The working culture at the police station was not one that I wanted to be a part of. If you didn't laugh along when they touched you up, or if you insisted on asking them to try and pronounce your name properly, you were instantly labelled 'difficult' and alienated from the group. Even my trousers marked me out to them as 'demanding special treatment'. I wasn't like the other girls, I 'couldn't have a laugh', so no one sat with me during refs (our name for a break), just as had been the case at Hendon. When they did talk to me it was usually to ask pointed questions like what I ate for breakfast at home.

'So what do you have then?'

'Cereal or toast.'

'So you don't just eat curry all the time?'

Perhaps that's why I was quieter, kept myself to myself. I knew that engagement meant putting up with wilful ignorance and sexual harassment. In some ways it was a blessing that they ostracized me. After a gruelling night shift, I didn't want to join them for drinks in the early hours, but thankfully they would never think to invite me. I was just grateful to get home.

'You weren't out on your own last night, were you?' Mum asked when I came in through the door in time for breakfast. This was the same mum who still got the bus to school with us when we were in sixth form.

'No,' I lied, 'I was in the office all night with the others.'

'Are the people you work with nice?' she asked.

'Yes, really nice,' I lied. 'They look after me.'

'I must come to your station some time, or you can invite them home,' she said.

The thought of Mum coming to the station was my worst nightmare. How could I introduce her to people who refused even to say my name properly? She would be horrified.

In the parade room each evening we were sent off in

pairs, except, more often than not, once I'd passed my street duties, I found myself patrolling alone. None of them wanted to patrol with me. This was one of the most dangerous areas of London, and I would be walking along dark streets at two or three o'clock in the morning, in all weathers, completely alone. Throughout the shift patrol cars would drive past me in the pouring rain, the officers waving and jeering from the inside.

Even the working girls – the prostitutes – seemed more concerned than my colleagues to see me patrolling alone on foot.

'What are you doing out here on your own?' they'd ask, seeming to miss the irony that they were doing exactly the same thing.

I asked myself then, what prompts a woman to go out at that time, to stand on street corners at night, in all weathers, having no idea whose car they're getting into and, most importantly, whether they were going to make it out again?

Throughout my life I had always had to work three times as hard as everyone else: firstly as a woman, and secondly as a woman of colour. My work at Leman Street would be no different. Where the white women in the station gained the respect of their colleagues by submitting to the 'banter', the way I tried to gain their respect was to put myself in ever more dangerous scenarios, though unlike my white colleagues I didn't always get the back-up. I knew the danger of walking the streets alone, so I stuck to the main roads, where I could be seen. I didn't want anyone back at the station to forget I was out there, so I did more vehicle checks, more road tax and insurance checks, more stops than any of my other colleagues, just so I had an excuse to radio in. When the CAD (Computer Aided Dispatch) room asked over the radio for units to take a call – a burglary, car theft, domestic disturbance or to assist another officer – it was always me who took the call first, assuring them I was in the neighbourhood even if it was right on the other side of the borough. I did it simply for something to do, for a reason to keep in touch with the control room. But despite the fact that this meant I was working twice as hard as everyone else, I still didn't earn the respect of my team. Still I was forced to patrol alone. I thought perhaps all probationers were treated like this, but as new probationers arrived, I saw how the others quickly made an assessment of them, and welcomed those who would 'fit' into the fold. One of the new recruits was a guy they called Wolfy. They liked him because he would go into great details about his sex life. I could see now that there were many things the team valued in an officer, and hard work seemed quite far down that list.

What I didn't realize was that they were still scheming about how to initiate me – something the other girls seemed to escape.

One night duty I arrived at the station and found it strange that after parade, rather than drifting off on their various duties, all the men seemed to be hanging around. I went to my pigeon-hole in the writing room – the room where we filled out our endless paperwork – where they were all congregated as if waiting for a meeting. I opened the tray with my name on it to check for any paperwork that had been left for me, and as I did so I was aware that the room had hushed behind me.

Inside my tray was a chunky A4 brown envelope. On

the front of it was my number and name: 269 Mehtab. I opened it, confused as to what might be inside. I stuffed my hand in and pulled out a rubber contraption, 6 or 7 inches in length. For a second I was utterly perplexed as to what it was, until I saw the on/off switch on the side and heard the sniggering behind me.

'Urgh.'

I shoved the vibrator back into the envelope and threw it on to the ground. I turned round to see every man in the room doubled over with laughter. Glaring at them I stormed out, making for the ladies' changing room.

I sat inside the cubicle, trying to process what they had done to me and why. Even from in there I could still hear them laughing. This was a power play by white male officers hoping for maximum impact, to remind me of my place. My choice in that split second had been to play along with them or become a laughing stock – what a choice for a woman who is just trying to get on with her job! Looking back, it just shows how scared they were of me. They needed to humiliate me to make themselves feel better.

When I finally emerged from the changing room I saw that the parade room was empty, the vibrator had gone from my tray and there were just one or two officers milling around as if nothing had happened. One of them came over to me.

'You shouldn't have had such a bad reaction,' he said. 'You should have just laughed it off.'

'It was disgusting,' I replied.

'You should have just made a joke of it, said "Oh thanks, I'll use it later."'

I stared at him as if we were speaking entirely different

languages, and perhaps we were. What he was saying to me was that this was the way things were done around here. He was telling me how I *should* behave if I wanted to do well in this station, if I wanted to be seen as 'one of them', if I wanted to be accepted. But the problem was, I didn't. I just wanted to be able to do the job I'd been trained for without being degraded.

I think, in some way, that day defined my time at Leman Street. I wasn't complicit in their sexism, I refused to listen to their dirty jokes and laugh at their locker-room banter, and I wouldn't allow the inspector to touch me inappropriately. All of that marked me out as different, and so my colleagues kept their distance from me. They didn't know how to handle me so instead I was isolated, labelled stroppy, difficult, unable to take a joke. It was *me* who should have reacted better, not them who needed to change their behaviour.

In many ways, perhaps minds had already been made up about me before I even arrived. It seemed my reputation had preceded me.

I had been stationed at Leman Street for a few months when Inspector 'Handy' asked to see me for my appraisal.

'I'm worried about you, Nidgit,' he said. 'You don't say much – you're very quiet.'

I looked straight at him, unsure where this conversation was going.

'You don't fit in,' he said, 'and I don't know if you can go out there and speak to men. What will you do if you have to touch a man?'

What? Just because I didn't allow him to put his hands on me meant that I wouldn't be able to touch a man in the course of arresting him? After more conversation I realized *exactly* what he was referring to. He knew that it was for religious reasons that I wore trousers and not a skirt, and so now he assumed – or someone had told him – that my religion forbade me from touching men too. I could just hear the sneering chatter between him and my sergeant at Hendon.

'But I've already made arrests and handcuffed them, so I'm not really sure what you mean, sir?' I told him.

'But can you handle yourself in a difficult situation?'

The ignorance of the team was more blatant than ever and I was once again reminded that the Met were ready for officers of colour in name only.

It was for this reason that I never told anyone when I was fasting. I knew that they had no cultural awareness or understanding of different faiths despite the fact they policed a large Muslim community. I didn't want to try to explain to them and then deal with their comments. They already thought I was weird; why would I volunteer any extra information just so that they could further ridicule me and my religion? When they were handing out doughnuts or cream buns I just politely refused, even when they insisted. I guessed I would just have to look ungrateful to them. I would break my fast alone in the ladies' changing room, and if suddenly assigned a call, I would have to leave my food and run. What was supposed to be a communal celebration, shared with friends, family and colleagues, was suddenly an isolated, rushed affair.

Over those first few months at Leman Street I noticed more and more how differently the male officers treated their female counterparts. I remember once attending a fight in a flat in Tower Hamlets. It was on the top floor in an estate not too dissimilar from the one I had grown up in in Hackney, and one after the other we raced up the stairwell to get to the top floor. But at each floor the men pulled us back by our uniforms and pushed past, determined to reach the fight before the women and then criticize us for not getting there fast enough – was that chivalry or sexism? By the smiles on their faces, they found it funny, so I would say the latter.

Another time I was patrolling in Stepney Green when a group of teenage boys ran past me. As they did, they whacked me on the back with some kind of stick, then ran off. The pain was so intense it made me stop still in the street.

I radioed into the control room, told them I'd been hit and gave them a description of the boys, and one of the area cars went looking for them, without luck. But by the time I got back to the station, my colleagues were questioning my account, or at least using it as an excuse to harass me.

'Take your shirt off and let's have a look then, Nidgit,' one of the white male PCs said.

The other men sniggered. Even the sergeant found it funny.

'No,' I protested.

Why did I have to prove that it had happened? If any other officer got hurt they would wrap them up in cotton wool, all the officers rallying round. When I got hurt they doubted my account unless I agreed to take my shirt off and show them the marks.

Worse than patrols on foot, I came to dread the night

shifts in the patrol car. You would have thought I would be grateful not to be out on the streets alone, but what car patrol often entailed was my male colleagues pulling up outside one of the nightclubs in the City, or Mile End Road, and watching the clubs turn out their clientele. They called it 'going to see the crumpet'. The male officers would watch from their cars, making lewd comments about the women who were coming out. I would sit there, uncomfortably, trying to move them on.

'Why?' they'd say. 'You can look at the men too.'

There wasn't much I could do to force them to keep driving, so instead I was stuck there while they picked women out of the crowd.

'Look at the state of that!' they'd say, pointing and laughing at one woman. 'She's a moose.'

I sank down in my seat and switched off.

'Look at her, she's a babe.'

'Phwoar, I would . . .'

'Lucky guy taking her home.'

Even the next day in the parade room the men would still be swapping notes about the women they'd seen.

'She was really sexy, did you see what she was wearing?'

'Not much at all!'

Listening to such comments from my male colleagues was something that simply became – quite literally – white noise to me.

The young female recruits I teach now tell me identical stories. Thirty years on and I'm still hearing the phrase 'looking at the crumpet'. The toxic culture prevails and has not been tackled from when I was a PC. Poor supervision is identified by Baroness Casey as a factor, and these individuals are enabled by the silent majority around them. If you challenge the way things are done then you are the problem; you're described as creating 'drama', as one female recruit told me.

In March 2018, an allegation was made internally within the Met Police that an officer had sex with a drunk woman at Charing Cross Police Station in central London. A three-year Independent Office for Police Conduct (IOPC) investigation followed which uncovered a toxic working environment and a culture of sexism, racism, bullying and homophobia led predominantly by fourteen Met officers working out of this station. The newspapers described the contents of the report as 'genuinely jaw-dropping', though perhaps it wasn't so shocking to those of us who had witnessed many similar incidents over the years. WhatsApp messages sent by a male officer to a female officer uncovered in the investigation included 'I would happily rape you', 'If I was single I would actually hate fuck you' and 'If I was single I would happily chloroform you'.

The Met apologized, and the group of male officers involved were disbanded. Some were fired, but not all of them. The IOPC then made fifteen recommendations including that the Met needed to publicly commit to a 'zero tolerance' position on sexism and misogyny. This was particularly key, as the report found that those who did not share the views, or partake in the 'banter', and especially those who challenged it, were 'ostracised, harassed and humiliated'.

Here is one case study example taken from Baroness Casey's review:

H says that hierarchies, initiation tests, bullying and humiliation of junior officers were rife in the unit. She says women were pressured to compete in food eating challenges to initiate them into the team, and described women being forced to eat whole cheesecakes until they would vomit. On one occasion she was told of a male officer being sexually assaulted in the showers as part of their own initiation, something she says officers would openly talk and joke about on the unit. Those who refused to participate were ostracised and considered 'not to be part of the team'.

Given my own experience, this was all far too familiar, and I'm sure a lot of other female officers would feel the same. Is it any wonder, then, that Baroness Casey's review found that 'women are not treated equally in the workforce, with new women recruits resigning at four times the rate of all probationers; and a third of Met women we surveyed reporting personally experiencing sexism at work, with 12% reporting directly experiencing sexual harassment or assault'?

It is shocking to me that the Met have allowed this 'toxic masculinity', as the IOPC described it, to flourish. The IOPC acknowledged in its own report that superiors allow this sexist 'banter' to go unchallenged, which only further empowers male officers to speak about women in this way.

But the issue is not just what women are supposed to accept in terms of their working life. It spills into the way male officers view women more generally, and it makes the public less safe as a result. The Met cannot expect that an officer who has sexually assaulted one of his own colleagues could take seriously a complaint by a member of the public about her own sexual assault.

The report recognized that women are woefully under-represented within the Met, with female officers comprising 31 per cent of police officers, compared to 51.5 per cent of the population. Although the number of new recruits has been rising steadily, the Met still take on twice as many male officers as women. Is it any wonder that toxic masculinity continues to dominate the service?

Baroness Casey's review stated that sexism was in plain sight on visits: 'We observed women being spoken over, put down and their views dismissed as inaccurate.' One woman reported to the review that when she was a victim of an unwanted touch by a colleague, witnessed by her sergeant, she was just told to 'stay out of his way'. Another woman working within the Met had this to say:

> The MPS (Metropolitan Police Service) is a male orientated and misogynistic environment filled with testosterone, notches on bed posts and conquests. From the outset of my service I have witnessed senior officers and supervisors prey on females like predators. There is a culture of hit lists, targets and trying to sleep with female officers and staff. Women are viewed as inferior and not truly belonging, being judged on looks and physical assets only. Only women who are either attractive or willing to have sex with colleagues are accepted. When a woman joins the police or is new to borough or team, they are immediately targeted by men competing to sleep with them. Attractive women are parachuted into posts or positions often simply

because someone who has taken a liking to them wants to gain an advantage over them. The way women dress is spoken about and [it] is deeply uncomfortable.

I had always thought, or hoped, that things weren't as blatant now as they had been for me three decades before, but it turned out that was not the case. It is true what one of the case studies states: if senior staff talk like this in front of new recruits, it teaches them that this is acceptable within the Met. These new recruits, who are the officers of the future, learn that these behaviours are OK, and such attitudes are therefore pervasive and enduring.

And, as I've said, if this is the culture within the station, isn't it likely it'll be applied out in public?

The Met's response to the IOPC report was typical: 'We do not believe there is a culture of misogyny in the Met . . . [In] an organisation of more than 44,000 people there will be a small number with attitudes and beliefs that are not welcome in the Met; we will challenge, educate and discipline as appropriate.' Once again, the narrative blamed 'a few bad apples' – a term that undermines and insults all those who have been the subject of misogyny, racism and homophobia within a system that has enabled and endorsed it. In reality, the orchard is crawling with maggots.

So what is the solution? The reason men feel an entitlement to speak this way about women, or behave this way towards women, is because the police are simply not being policed. There is a system in place to stop this kind of behaviour but the process and procedures are ineffective. They lack sanctions, accountability and oversight. Inappropriate behaviour is enabled and endorsed by the

Met by virtue of this inaction. I've known of cases myself where probationers have reported their sergeants for hitting on them during their working day. I supported one young woman who did this and when she didn't respond to his advances he turned nasty, blocking her courses and career development. He was removed from the team temporarily, but he was returned to the same team while the investigation was still ongoing. How can the Met be safeguarding other women when they have placed him back on the same team? This is red flag behaviour, but where are the mechanisms for capturing this going forward?

Even when women's reports are taken seriously, it still takes on average 400 days for the matter to be investigated. What does that tell the perpetrator about how seriously these allegations against him are being taken?

I agree with the IOPC that the Met need to have a zero tolerance policy on this, to commit to it publicly, but most importantly to see it through. When a woman reports harassment, she is often left on the same team as her perpetrator. The Met need to remove these men who have multiple allegations made against them. If it were me and someone came to me with a complaint, I would investigate it thoroughly and quickly. If it transpired that the person they were accusing had been accused before, I would suspend him immediately pending the investigation. The Met might say they do that, but it is often easier to disbelieve the woman than it is to hold the man accountable. This is true and concerning in all areas of life, but it certainly shouldn't be that way within our police forces.

During my probationary days, I was always determined to prove everyone else wrong. In fact, I silently dared them to underestimate me on account of my gender – I would show them. Whenever we received a call over our radios that one of our officers was attending a fight, the whole team would rush to back them up. We knew how quickly these things could get out of hand, but while the men had the brute strength to deal with incidents like that, they weren't always the best people to handle them. One of the officers was nicknamed 'Punchy' because he didn't so much extinguish a fight as ignite it. If he attended the call, he would end up getting into the fight because he just didn't know how to deal with people. I noticed a lot of the men were like that; it was a macho thing, a toxic masculinity; they felt they had something to prove – not so dissimilar to the men who were starting the fights in the first place. There is a very fine line between being assertive enough to calm a situation and being so aggressive that you make it worse.

I had probably been on the team for a year when one day I was patrolling in the police van with a male colleague. For some reason he decided to stop a car and asked the driver to get out. The woman with the driver was clearly intoxicated, or perhaps just very agitated that her boyfriend had been stopped. While my colleague radioed in to check the paperwork on the driver, his girlfriend was screaming and yelling abuse at us. She had been told to remain inside the car, but kept getting out. I could see this situation could very easily spiral out of control, and it was showing on my colleague's face. He was having trouble focusing on the driver who was also getting aggressive. We shared a glance, and without a word I went round to the passenger side. The woman was out of the car now, mounting the kerb, screaming.

She was of large build, gesticulating wildly, shouting and swearing. Other members of the public were stopping to stare.

I knew I had to find a way of calming her down; arresting her would only make the situation worse. Of course I was scared: she was bigger than me, broader than me, and had worked herself into a wired, unreasonable state.

'I'm going to need to ask you to lower your tone,' I said, taking a step towards her.

She paused for a minute, assessing perhaps how I was going to stop her if she didn't. In situations like that, even if you don't feel confident, it is a matter of faking it, of speaking with authority, not aggression (a fine line that my male colleagues often didn't seem able to navigate). I stepped closer to her until my face was inches away from hers, looking her straight in the eye.

'If you do not calm down, I'm going to have to arrest you, which will make the situation more difficult for everyone.'

She was quiet, just for a second or two but long enough for me to spot a distinct change in her body language.

'Now, get back into the car and sit quietly while my colleague deals with your friend.'

Incredibly, she did as I said. The officer I was working with was clearly impressed, forgetting for a second that he was meant to be writing out a ticket. The woman sat there in the car staring ahead, calm now, resigned to let us do our job.

When we got back to Leman Street my colleague was full of praise for me. 'She handled that mad woman really well,' he told anyone who would listen, and for the first time they did listen. It seemed another man giving me the nod, the seal of approval, made all the difference. I was pleased that my hard work was finally being recognized, but couldn't shake a feeling of indignation. Why was it up to a man to decide my worth?

'Yeah, Nidgit can really handle herself.'

Another time we attended a pub fight at a proper old-fashioned East End boozer, the Blind Beggar. All units attended and I ran on foot, wanting to be there first as always. When I arrived, the area car crew were already getting out of the car and I could hear the sirens of the other cars on their way. Even from the street we could hear it was chaos inside the pub. It seemed as if every customer in there was throwing punches, bar stools, glasses – it felt more like the Wild West than Whitechapel.

I hadn't got more than a few yards inside the pub when I felt something hit the side of my hat with some force – it must have been a glass. It bounced off me, and in the time that I was distracted, someone jumped on me, hitting me repeatedly. I managed to spin round to face the man who was attacking me (all these years on, I can't remember what he looked like but I can still remember the alcohol on his breath) and a moment later I was on the floor, fighting to get this man off me and get his hands in cuffs. I managed to sit on him and grab his arm as two colleagues came to my aid.

It took a long time to get that pub under control again. I was the only female officer there that night and afterwards I wore it like a badge of honour.

'Nidgit's all right,' my male colleagues said once we were bundling everyone we had arrested into the police van. 'She doesn't mind getting stuck in.'

If my femininity would not work for them, I had to prove I was macho to be accepted. I didn't see the other WPCs putting themselves in the same danger I did, and they were treated more daintily, as if they were fragile. I think the colour of my skin saw to it that I was not seen like that. Where my white female colleagues were accepted so readily, I had to go above and beyond for a hint of recognition. I was not alone in this. Female officers of colour commented in the Casey review that in order to prove themselves they needed to work twice as hard as their white counterparts.

These moments were a turning point for me at Leman Street. The others eased up a little and began to treat me with less suspicion because 'one of theirs' had said I was 'one of them'. I still didn't join them for after-work drinks but they left me alone after that. They were suddenly like the school bullies who leave you alone once you stand up for yourself. Though, sadly, their name for me didn't change.

I tolerated my time at Leman Street, but I was never happy there. I loved the work but even after I'd earned a degree of respect I still felt othered, isolated, different and weird. Unfortunately I had to complete my two years' probation before I was even able to apply for a transfer.

Our posts rotated between patrolling on foot, patrolling in the car, being posted in the van, and taking our turn in the station office, either at Leman Street or Arbour Square. I was often posted to Arbour Square which was a quieter station and so it became a bit of a hangout for officers who wanted to stop for refs during patrol as there were no senior management there. There was, however, a cleaner called Maggie who would bring us all sorts of sweets and snacks. 'I need to look after my boys,' she'd say as she set down a tray of crisps and fruit. The men loved being fussed over by her. She was a lovely old lady, a real East Ender. When it was her birthday everyone chipped in and bought her a microwave. This was the late eighties, and not every household had one, so she was delighted.

There was something I liked about shifts covering the station office at Arbour Square, dealing with the odd member of the public who came in to report a crime, or those answering their bail conditions. Perhaps it was the break it provided from the rest of the team at Leman Street. Two years went by, and though I'd passed my probation, I had still not gelled with any of my colleagues, male or female. It was exhausting always to feel on edge around them. And so when I saw that the Met were launching a pilot to set up their first dedicated Domestic Violence Unit, and that it would be based at Arbour Square, I decided to apply.

3

Arbour Square

Arbour Square Police Station is a redbrick three-storey building on the corner of Aylward Street and East Arbour Street in Stepney. It has now been redeveloped into residential apartments, but before that it enjoyed a long history with the Metropolitan Police, whose officers moved in there in the mid-nineteenth century and stayed for 150 years. The most famous prisoners housed on the site were the Kray Twins, who ruled much of the East End of London in the 1960s.

When I arrived at Arbour Square to begin my new role in the early nineties, none of us knew that its time with the Met was drawing to a close, and that by the following decade it would be occupied by squatters. For now, it was the site of my new department – the first Domestic Violence Unit pilot scheme in the Met.

Up until that point, the Metropolitan Police had viewed and dealt with domestic violence in a very different way from how it's done now. It was, and perhaps remains, unlike other crimes, very much a case of he said/she said. Most often when I was working on the response team and we received a call to attend a 'domestic', we were instructed to 'square it up', which was code for making the problem go away. That meant, more often than not, that no action would be taken. We would attend the address, our presence alone often neutralizing the situation, and we would separate the couple – a male colleague often taking the man into one room, me taking the woman into another. In turn, my colleague and I would listen to six of one in one room, half a dozen in another, then leave them both with a warning that, should we have to return, arrests would be made. I would always take my time dealing with domestic incidents, to the annoyance of my colleagues who would say 'Hurry up, Nidgit, we've got other calls.' But I wanted to listen and understand what women were experiencing and consider how we could help.

Looking back now, I shudder at how little we knew then about domestic abuse. There were houses we returned to time and time again, but we rarely arrested anyone; it perhaps wasn't thought to be worth the paperwork. Instead we 'squared it up', just as we were told, and made the problem go away. 'She just got a bit gobby,' my male colleagues would often say when we left, 'and then he got a bit gobby.' To them it was as simple as that. What was the point in bringing people in and charging them when the same thing would happen the next day, or the next? Other people's relationships were not the business of the Met to police – or at least that's what people thought back then.

But the Met now wanted to take a different approach to policing domestic violence. They recognized that women were being killed in their homes. Eyes were turning to the Met, asking what they had done wrong and why they hadn't stepped in earlier. Something had to be done; it needed to be dealt with holistically with partner organizations that could offer longer-term support to victims.

This new Domestic Violence Unit would be a joint pilot programme between Leman Street and Bethnal Green Police Stations, with me heading up our unit at Arbour Square, and another woman, Maria, working out of Bethnal Green. Gone were the days of working night shifts. Instead, in Arbour Square, I could work a more respectable nine-to-five. But what my job did do was make it easier for the officers on shifts. It was no longer their problem to 'square up', it was mine. If they attended a domestic, they would pass the details on to me to follow up, and I would get in touch to find out more about what the victims had been experiencing and to put them in touch with other people who could help. The hands of my male colleagues were rinsed of responsibility, and I think for an awful lot of them that was just the way they liked it.

It seemed to me, new in the job, that one of the first things I needed to do was forge relationships between the police and the local women's refuges and other support organizations. After all, these were the people who were on the frontline of working with victims of domestic violence. It was they who knew the full extent of what we were dealing with and how we could do things more effectively. None of these refuges had ever had much interest or support from the police, so they welcomed me in and appreciated my questions and determination to figure out what the Met could do for victims.

I started working with Southall Black Sisters, a non-profit organization that was originally established to focus on the struggle of Asian women against racism but increasingly became involved in defending the rights of Asian women who were victims of domestic violence. I remember how my white colleagues judged the homes of people who looked like me and my family – families who would often live in poverty, or with several generations squeezed into a small flat. We were, after all, working in one of London's poorest boroughs. Often the houses smelt of spices, and I noticed how my colleagues wrinkled their noses, or made comments about the smell as we left. I could see some officers often judging the way these people lived, but stopping short of making comments in front of me.

In the same way that Asian households were 'alien' to white police officers, so were the problems they contained, and due to the mistrust between the Asian community and the police, many women had nowhere to turn to. Back then, the East End of London was populated by many Muslim and Asian communities so my background was helpful in earning their trust. My plan was to create partnerships between domestic violence organizations and the police. This meant organizations like Southall Black Sisters suddenly had someone within the police they could refer victims to, and likewise I could offer to put victims in touch with charities like theirs.

I liked this new part of my job, of building

relationships, of negotiating with members of the community and figuring out how we could work together in a way that was mutually beneficial. It seemed to me that liaising with the community was where a lot of my skills lay, and it probably helped that I looked like the people the force were serving in that area. It built trust. I'd never really enjoyed stopping cars going through red lights, or patrolling on my own at night, and this was meaningful work. I was connecting with women on a one-to-one basis, getting to know them slowly, getting to understand their stories.

After a referral had been made to me by an officer after a domestic violence disturbance, I would invite victims to my office at Arbour Street to come and chat with me, to help them take the next steps, to see if they needed help to leave their partner or ask them if they wanted to press charges. I kept an index of people who were referred to me by officers, and followed up with them to see what else we could do as an organization, not just once but over a period of time, making notes after every phone call. I think that alone helped women to feel safer – and the victims I dealt with were overwhelmingly women, the perpetrators almost always men.

It was my job to follow up on every call that officers made when an allegation of domestic abuse had been reported to me. I would have the bare minimum in terms of detail: name, address, and what the victim had told the attending officer had occurred. My first contact with a victim would be by letter, and if I didn't hear from her I would go and knock on her door. I wasn't in uniform then – it wasn't necessary for the work I was doing – but I soon learnt that going to someone's home could often put them in more danger. I remember the first few times I turned up and knocked at doors, having no idea of the dynamic that was at play on the other side. The men answered, demanding to know who I was, and why I was asking for their wife. They were intimidating, reeking of control, and often alcohol. I could see why the women involved found these men intimidating.

I quickly learnt that it was best for women to come and see me at the station, though I knew how difficult it was for some of them to get away. Often their every move was monitored, and of course back then, unlike today, coercive control was not a crime (it was only added to the Domestic Abuse Act in 2021).

One contact I was given by teams was a lady who lived in Jamaica Street with her husband. I went and knocked on her door and an angry-looking man answered.

'Is she in?' I asked breezily, as if I was a regular visitor to their house.

'Who are you?' he said.

'Oh, I'm just a friend.'

'Well, I don't know you.'

He slammed the door in my face.

She called me at the police station that afternoon, telling me that he had given her hell for me turning up like that, and promised she would visit me at my office. Ilsa was in her sixties, an Austrian lady who had come over to help with the war effort. She'd been with her husband forty years, but what she described sounded nothing like a healthy marriage. He monitored everything: who she saw, who she spoke to, where she went, how much money she had. He stripped her of her personality when she was inside that house, but when she visited me at

Arbour Square with her little bichon frise, Dinky, she was a different woman. She was alive, exuberant, and I loved listening to her old stories of when she came over to England.

'I'll have to get back,' she would say suddenly, putting down her tea. 'He'll wonder where I am.'

There was nothing I could do as a police officer to help her. Her husband wasn't hitting her – thankfully – and at that time we didn't understand the controlling nature of abuse and it certainly wasn't a crime. Back then, domestic abuse was only thought of as black eyes and bruises. All I could do was support her, but I couldn't make use of the law to get her away from a controlling husband. When coercive control was finally criminalized in 2021, I thought back to Ilsa, and wished we could've done more for her at the time.

I learnt a lot from my time at Arbour Square, the biggest thing being how difficult it was for women to come forward. I had heard all the clichés from my colleagues on teams: 'If it's that bad, why doesn't she just leave?' I perhaps would have said those things myself once, but talking to these women, spending time with them, showed me why they couldn't 'just' leave. There is often economic control. Men take charge of the finances, while these women have no money, no jobs, no means of walking out of their relationships. They are often isolated from their support networks – family, friends, neighbours. There were often language barriers too. I met countless women like my own mother who didn't speak English, or were brought to this country to marry their husbands where they found themselves reliant on them for everything.

One Bengali woman came into the station with her two daughters, who were about eight or nine. She couldn't speak English, but there was clearly something she needed me to know about her marriage and so her daughters sat and patiently translated everything she said. I immediately had an affinity with them. They reminded me of me and my siblings when I was that age and we had to go with Mum to the Housing Association or to the market to get her shopping. This lady's husband was beating her, and it was harrowing to hear the daughters describe these incidents from their mother's own words. What was even worse was that over the months, when their mother disappeared out of the room to use the toilet, they started confiding in me about their father sexually abusing them. Clearly we would need to intervene, but not in the way that the mother had expected. I involved CID (the Criminal Investigation Department – commonly known as the detectives) and social services, the father was arrested, the other children in the household questioned and the whole family turned upside down. It was traumatic for all of them, especially as the mother hadn't had any idea that her daughters were suffering too. The father was eventually prosecuted and went to prison.

The women I met didn't immediately open up to me. At first they would insist that they were all right, that there was nothing they needed from the police. Coming from the council estates myself, I understood their distrust, though it created a barrier between us. Sometimes, though, days or even weeks later, they would come and find me in my office. Slowly they would begin to trust me when I told them that they could get an injunction that would prevent their partner from going near them again. It was tough work trying to help women so broken, knowing that they would more than likely return to the men who had broken them. I had to accept that women can feel paralysed in their relationships. It might not be on that occasion that they felt strong enough to leave. It might be the next, it might be never. All I could do was let these women know that staying with an abusive man wasn't their only option.

For all the women who felt they weren't able to get out, there were also women who, after spending a lot of time with me, finally felt able to leave their partners and I put them in touch with support services that helped them do that. It was on these occasions that I felt a real sense of achievement. I recognized that this was one of the best parts of policing – really making a difference. Unfortunately, such is the power that the perpetrator wields over the victim, they would often end up returning.

I was shopping in Stratford one Saturday morning when I saw a woman I had been helping to find a place in a refuge. I had been arranging a court date for her to serve her husband with an injunction, and there she was walking out of Sainsbury's with him. I stopped and stared. They looked so happy, *she* looked happy, happier than she had ever been as she sat in my office beside a box of tissues, pulling down her jumper to hide the purpling fingerprint marks around her wrist. To anyone else seeing them in that busy high street, they looked like any other couple. Other than me, no one in the vicinity would know that he had pulled out her hair from her scalp, thrown her from one side of the living room to another, or threatened to burn her with the iron she was pressing his shirts with.

She saw me and I just smiled, and we both looked away as if we didn't know each other.

That moment taught me a difficult lesson. A woman will only leave when she is ready, when the switch flicks and she realizes that she has to get out. This is usually when the children are in danger.

A few months later that same woman turned up at Arbour Square and asked for me. This time her hands were not shaking. This time she didn't need the box of tissues. Instead she had something else in her eyes – defiance.

'I've had enough, get him out,' she told me.

I still bumped into colleagues from Leman Street as they were sometimes posted to the station office at Arbour Square. I think, after I had left teams, they saw a different side to me. The same male colleague who told me that I handled the vibrator incident badly commented, 'I'm really impressed, this job is meant for you.'

I smiled back at him, curious about why men feel that women need their seal of approval. Mostly, though, I knew that my former colleagues were grateful for what I was doing because it meant that they didn't have to handle domestics themselves. No officer received training with regard to domestic abuse, and none of them understood the psychology of it back then.

I had been working in the unit for a few months when Maria joined at the Bethnal Green station. Maria was a woman with a personality as busy as her curly blonde hair. She was in her late twenties and had been an officer for ten years. She was also married to one of the police officers from where she had been based.

Between us we made a formidable team, building trust across the whole Tower Hamlets borough. We hadn't been given a budget for setting up the Domestic Violence Unit so we had to beg and borrow everything we got to make an office within the station comfortable and homely enough for women to feel comfortable visiting us. Often I used to kit it out from my own pocket, buying soft chairs from a second-hand shop, or a kettle and cups from Woolworths, and even asking local businesses for donations.

Maria and I divided the borough between Leman Street and Bethnal Green, me taking the calls in my area and she in hers. We discussed the cases together, however, and often went to arrest or serve injunctions on men together. Even though it wasn't part of our remit, we would often interview perpetrators when we brought them into custody because we knew the cases so well.

We were working in the early nineties, which was a time when it was still legal to rape your wife (it would be 1993 that would see a change in the law). Often the officers dealing with incidents like these were still in that mindset, still believing that a woman was the property of her husband. Of course – why would they think any different when even the law told them the same?

We saw some difficult cases during my time on the Domestic Violence Unit: women who were trapped at home with children, completely dependent on men who would not allow them to leave the house, who did the shopping so their wives weren't even in control of what they ate or what they wore. But I also came to understand that within those four walls they did, to a certain extent, have some agency over their own lives. They lived in their own homes, they had status as married women, and that was a lot to give up in their community. That was the bit that was hard to pull them away from, to take their children from their toys and move them into shared accommodation, into one room for them and their multiple children. It was never as simple as 'they should just leave' and my job was never to persuade them to, just to let them know what support they could expect from the police and other services if they ever did.

I found that it was often the strongest women that abusers tried to break. I remember one of them in particular, Diane. She came to me via a referral and I spoke to her on the phone, asking her to come and meet me in my office at Arbour Square.

'I can't leave the flat,' she told me. She had three children and she explained it was impossible for her to leave them.

Instead I agreed I would go to her – something I wouldn't usually do.

'He won't be here, he'll be at work,' she said, assuring me he would never come home in the middle of the day.

Diane lived on a housing estate in Stepney, in a tower block. I took the lift up to the sixteenth floor. Inside Diane's tiny two-bedroom flat everything was somehow neat and tidy despite the fact she had three children under four. A dark hallway led to the living room and as I walked past the bedrooms I saw three little boys playing with Lego.

'Be good while I speak to the lady,' she told them.

In their living room whose big windows looked out across the east London skyline we sat down and I pulled out my paperwork. I took notes as Diane told me a little about the history of the relationship, and paused every so often, putting down my pen, as she cried, reliving some of the abuse she had experienced. Here was a woman who, like so many others, was putting on a brave face to the world and to her children while inside she was at breaking point.

'I want to leave now,' she told me. 'I don't want the boys to grow up thinking this is normal.'

I told her about some of the support organizations that could help her and she agreed to let me put them in touch with her. We also started talking about whether there were grounds for getting an injunction which would keep her and the boys safe.

Only about half an hour into our chat we heard a key in the door.

Diane looked at me. The fear in her face was instant.

'It's him.'

I quickly gathered up my paperwork just as he came through the front door. Diane's body language changed instantly, and she was standing as he came into the living room, her arms folded tightly across her chest.

He looked at me.

'Who the fuck are you?'

Diane's husband wasn't a particularly well-built man, he was rangy, skinny, and had tattoos that snaked all the way up both arms, but his body language was aggressive and the atmosphere in the flat had changed.

He turned to his wife. 'Who's she?'

On teams I had dealt with aggressive men. I knew I

must keep calm, appear confident, even if I didn't feel it on the inside.

'I've come here to speak with Diane,' I said.

'Oh yeah, what about?'

For a second I was silent. I noticed Diane's hands shaking.

'I'm from housing,' I lied, trying to think of something. 'I've come to talk to her about the flat.'

'Yeah, well, you didn't ask me, did you?' He was moving towards me jabbing his finger through the air as I shuffled backwards. 'So you can get out of my fucking flat.'

Diane took a step towards him. 'Leave her alone,' she said. 'I asked her to come.'

He turned on her. 'You didn't ask me if someone could come here and talk about my flat.'

Over the last few months I'd heard women talk about how frightened they were, how the atmosphere in their home could change in a second. This was perhaps the first time I had experienced it for myself.

He was suddenly up in Diane's face. She flinched as he prodded her.

'You didn't tell me anyone was coming here, to my house.'

'I'm sorry,' she said.

And that's when he pushed her, hard in the chest. Again, again. She stumbled backwards and fell to the floor. That's when I stood up. I had no choice then but to intervene, even though I was aware that giving away my identity could put us both in danger.

I took a step towards him purposefully. 'I'm a police officer,' I said.

He was silent for just a split second while my words sank in. I hoped that it might calm him down, but instead his eyes flashed, angry.

'You said you were from housing, you lying bitch.'

He pushed me then, and I stumbled backwards. Diane got up, tried to stop him. The situation was suddenly looking very dangerous. I heard one of the boys starting to cry.

As Diane tried to shove him away from me, I grabbed my bag and pressed the emergency button on my radio, calling to all units. Even if my colleagues were in the area, it would still take a few minutes for them to get up to the sixteenth floor. I needed to do something to try and calm things down, but what? I didn't have time to think, or even to be scared. I jumped up, concerned for Diane's safety.

'You need to stop,' I told him, mustering my most authoritative voice. 'I will leave, I promise. But I will only leave when I know that Diane is all right.'

This wasn't true. He'd already assaulted both of us and would need to be arrested, but I knew it would buy me the vital minutes I needed until back-up arrived.

The children were still crying in the other room.

'Diane, go into the other room with the boys,' I said.

'Oi, you don't tell her what to do in my—'

And then I heard them.

'Police!'

My colleagues burst straight into the living room and restrained Diane's husband just as he was coming at me again. Within seconds they had him on the floor in cuffs. Finally I could breathe, but I knew deep down that this could have ended badly. I should never have agreed to come to Diane's flat – for her sake or mine. I should have found a way for her to come to the station, and I absolutely shouldn't have attended her flat alone.

Between 2022 and 2023, domestic abuse-related crimes accounted for 11 per cent of all crimes that the Met dealt with, up by 9.6 per cent compared to figures from 2017–18. This rise might be down to the fact that there is more awareness of what abuse is and what it looks like in society on the whole, and also perhaps that victims might be more likely to come forward in what seems like a more supportive landscape. Though the shockingly low figure indicating what happens after they have reported the abuse doesn't exactly inspire confidence. Fewer than 7 per cent of the 95,000 domestic abuse-related crimes reported to the Met in 2022 resulted in a charge. Of those charged, 66.4 per cent of those that reached court resulted in a conviction, which means that around just 4 per cent of those 95,000 people who reported domestic abuse will see their abuser held accountable in a court of law. Out of all forces in England and Wales, the Met have the most woeful figures, which is some cause for concern when two women are killed every week by a current or former partner in England and Wales.

While the Met still struggle to police domestic abuse across London, it's worth looking at how it polices the offence within its own ranks. The number of misconduct allegations against officers (both by the public and internally) has increased steadily over the last decade, rising from sixty-three in 2013 to 166 in 2022. This could be down to a number of factors, though the Met believe it is due mostly to victims having the confidence to come forward. However, once they do come forward, the outcomes are disappointing. In Baroness Casey's review, she pointed out that misconduct allegations involving domestic violence are 'half as likely to receive a case to answer decision, when compared to all case types'. Otherwise they are dismissed as no case to answer.

In fact, the figures are quite shocking. Seventy-seven per cent of allegations are found to be 'no case to answer' and go uninvestigated, 9 per cent of cases are 'discontinued' and only 14 per cent are found to be cases to answer. Furthermore, Baroness Casey's review remarked on the fact that in domestic abuse misconduct cases, 'interviews with all victims and suspects were not always taken'. She described this as 'a surprise and [a] major concern'.

Investigators were also told that forces rarely shared information if an officer was arrested outside the Met area when, according to Casey, this information should be shared 'as a matter of routine'. This meant that if Met officers were arrested in their own home for domestic violence, or anything else, their superiors often weren't aware.

So what is going on? We already know that the Met are viewed by many as a boys' club, and more specifically in my experience a white boys' club. The Centre for Women's Justice reported that the partners of serving officers 'feel doubly powerless. They experience the powerlessness that most domestic abuse victims experience, but in addition their abuser is part of the system intended to protect them.'

Nowhere was this more apparent than in the case of David Carrick, the Met officer who was jailed for life after pleading guilty to eighty-five charges including rapes, assaults, false imprisonment and coercive control. In an anonymous interview with Sky News, his former wife claimed that she had faced an 'uphill battle' with West Yorkshire Police to get them to take her allegations against him seriously. 'It makes you feel worthless,' she told a reporter, 'and when you have come from that sort of relationship it kind of reinforces that feeling that my words don't matter. If anything I wouldn't feel safe calling 999 because I wouldn't trust they would ever bother coming at all.'

In March 2020, the Centre for Women's Justice submitted a Police Super-Complaint into the failures of forces nationally to address police-perpetrated domestic violence. The results of this super-complaint found evidence of police perpetrators trying to stop the victim from reporting to the police, drawing on their status as police officers to undermine the victim. During her own review, Baroness Casey also 'heard of cases in the Met where friends and superiors had closed ranks around the police suspect to protect them'.

In all other walks of life you can accept that there are a certain number of 'perks to the job' – for example, if you work in a restaurant you might get some free food, in a shop you might get a discount – but the thought that senior officers in the Met might be turning a blind eye to protect an abusive friend is sickening. Though sadly it's not at all surprising to me because I have seen time after time the way that white male officers close ranks.

After David Carrick's offences came to light and as part of the Met's Rebuilding Trust Programme, the force conducted Operation Rainier, a review of its sexual misconduct cases. This operation involved investigating all live sexual misconduct and domestic abuse claims (313 cases) plus a 'dip sample' of a hundred cases over the past ten years. What I find most shocking is the fact that 9 per cent of individuals who later faced complaints already had similar allegations against them even at the point of vetting to join the Met. The Met are willingly allowing these 'perpetrators' into the force. The operation also found that 85 per cent of the dip sample of a hundred cases resulted in no further action, and in 31 per cent of misconduct cases the victim was not contacted because they had previously withdrawn or not supported the criminal investigation. But anyone who has any experience of domestic violence knows that the psychology of this type of crime means that many victims are afraid to pursue or support an investigation against the perpetrator of their abuse. Such is the strength of the fear they wield against victims – and that must be ten-fold when your partner is a police officer.

If the police are not policing abusers internally, how on earth can the public be expected to believe that they will take their allegations seriously? Baroness Casey certainly found this a cause for concern:

> The Met's data, and its own review of misconduct and criminal investigations into police perpetrated domestic and sexual violence, indicates a worrying level of complacency about the risks posed by police officers who prey on officers and members of the public.
>
> It has not recognised that such men (and it is largely men) may be attracted to policing in the first place due to the power it gives them, or that predatory and repeat behaviour is a feature of such crime, or that the control they exert means that victims are less likely to report.

So what is the answer? For me, it is *extremely* concerning that the abusers are not rooted out during the vetting process. At present each force has its own appetite for risk, and therefore sets its own threshold as to what offences it considers makes a person not fit for police work. Some have a higher threshold than others and tolerate abusers, and once in, there is no monitoring process or risk of mitigation and they get lost in the system. There is no consistency between regional police forces in an area where a national solution is sorely needed. The Home Secretary needs to legislate a minimum standard for forces.

It is no wonder to me that serving officers at Charing Cross Police Station felt comfortable sending each other WhatsApp messages bragging about 'smacking' their own wives. Through their previous inaction, the Met have not told those men that their behaviour is not welcome in their organization. In fact they're the very men they picked to serve and protect.

No man who is an abuser should be considered for a role within the Met. No man who has had allegations made against him should be able to continue in his role. Forces should be compelled by law to share data about allegations made against police officers either inside or outside of working hours and there needs to be a national database to achieve that. If men are bullies at home then that gives a good indication of how they will be at work, and how they will behave with the general public – they may even have been drawn to policing work for that reason. Supervisors of officers who have had allegations of domestic abuse, sexual misconduct or discrimination against them should be alerted so that they can monitor them and reduce their access to the public while they are being investigated. And we need to let go of this idea that if women who come forward later drop the complaint, it means it didn't happen. All allegations should be investigated.

The pilot programme run by Maria and me was a great success and would go on to form what would become permanent dedicated units working to police violence against women and girls. I'm proud of the part that I played in the eighteen months that I was there.

We were given the time to get to know these women, to build their cases, and often to build trust. The more they opened up about historical abuse, the stronger our cases became and the more we could help them.

Back then, Maria and I did not receive any training in terms of what domestic abuse is or what it looks like, and that definition has changed over time as people understood more about the psychology of abuse. Today those old Domestic Violence Units are now called Community Safety Units (CSU) and all police working within them are specifically trained to deal with domestic abuse whether they are officers or detectives. In 2021, the Metropolitan Police Service trained 6,700 frontline uniformed officers in Domestic Abuse Matters training. There's still a long way to go, but I'm invigorated by the steps that have been taken since my time on the programme.

I left Arbour Square when I felt that I had taken the pilot programme as far as I could. I was ready for a new challenge, and when an opportunity came up in a specialized unit I decided to apply for it.

4

Charing Cross

Charing Cross Police Station was designed in Georgian times by the famous architect Decimus Burton, the same man who was responsible for many of London's foremost landscapes and buildings. It was originally the site of Charing Cross Hospital, but was taken over by the Metropolitan Police in the early 1990s, and not long after that it became the station at which I was based.

The Clubs and Vice Unit was founded in the 1930s and based at West End Central Police Station. The unit was primarily formed to deal with prostitution, but the dark underbelly of London's Soho – particularly after the Second World War – meant that it was expanded over the years to include nightclubs, licensing laws, gaming, casinos and pornography. The remit of Clubs and Vice was to perform covert operations, and this was what had appealed to me, and why I had applied to join. But the unit had its own history of corruption. In the early 1970s it was discovered that a well-known pornographer had paid seventeen detectives in the obscene publications squad to look the other way. The entire squad (in total more than twenty detectives) was disbanded and replaced with uniformed officers who were thought to be less easily corrupted than CID.

I arrived at Charing Cross Police Station in the mid-nineties for my first shift as a police constable with Clubs and Vice. New recruits to Clubs and Vice were sent to Hendon to do a day's decoy training. It felt good to be returning to Hendon as a fully fledged officer without those new-recruit nerves. Back in the old classrooms it was interesting work. We did role-play scenarios that were set up in each room to give us a feel of the type of work we might be doing. Our roles in Clubs and Vice would often require decoy work, so we needed to practise thinking on our feet, talking our way into situations – and potentially out of them. At Hendon, experienced undercover officers would play the roles of the drug dealers, and often these men had bigger egos than the criminals themselves, so the scenarios felt frighteningly realistic.

I remember going up for my first practice scenario, watched over by my fellow classmates.

'Can you serve me up?' I asked, approaching the two men who were posing as dealers.

They didn't even look up.

I shuffled from foot to foot, unsure what to do next.

'Who the fuck are you?' one of them said finally. 'And what is it that you think I do? I don't fucking know you. Fuck off.'

I stared back at my classmates. Their faces looked as

blank as I guessed my own was, but I could see what they were teaching us: that we would need to earn the trust of people out on the streets. I tried again, attempting to use my charm to engage them in conversation a bit first. Slowly, I felt the two men warming to me. I was clearly doing something right. It is incredible that even in a classroom situation you can feel so intimidated.

'So, can you help me?' I asked again.

'Sure, I'll serve you,' the other one said, 'but I like that jacket you're wearing.'

'What?'

'Yeah, your jacket, I want it. So if you want to get served, you're going to have to give me your jacket.'

I was stumped again. We were not wired up, but I knew that in real life there was a chance I might be. Still, refusing to take my jacket off might ruin the entire operation. In that moment, it was the only way I could think to get those fictional drugs, so I did it.

Afterwards the class discussed what happened. The instructors pointed out that I was wrong to hand over my jacket for that very reason: in real life it could've completely blown my cover. It was a lesson for us all. We did other scenarios, over and over again, in turn. Each of us was pushed and pressed, having to deal with various complex situations we couldn't even have dreamt up. We watched the instructors act out a similar scenario to the one I had done previously. Again, the dealer asked for his jacket. 'Nah bruv, my mum bought me this jacket before she died, I can't give this away to no one.' The instructor glanced at me, watching for the flicker of recognition to land on my face.

I returned to Charing Cross feeling excited about

deploying all these new skills. The decoy training had been tough and I felt proud for passing. A few weeks later, me and another girl were dispatched to carry out a decoy operation in Electric Avenue in Brixton. Sometimes police training involved learning things the hard way, and that was definitely one of those occasions. We turned up to the station for our briefing and met the team in our ordinary clothes, newly laundered as usual, our hair freshly washed. The officers there just laughed at us.

'You're not going to fit in around here,' they said. 'You're too clean for a street buy.'

The key to decoy work was to blend in, to look the part as well as act it. From that day forward we always kept a grubby set of clothing in our lockers. On sting days we remembered not to brush our hair, not even to wash.

'You're going out to work like that?' Mum said, as I left one morning.

How could I tell her that her obedient Muslim daughter was off to east London to try and buy drugs?

Back at Charing Cross, the team I was posted into was small, just one sergeant and six of us officers. Our night shifts started at 6 p.m. and finished around 2 a.m., when even trade for the working girls slowed down and London was littered with drunks, empty glass bottles and takeaway cartons. From 6 p.m. to 8 p.m. each shift we'd be doing our paperwork at the station, writing up intelligence we had gathered from the night before or planning operations, and by eight o'clock we'd be out on the streets.

The sergeant was ex-Territorial Support Group (a unit of the Met that specialized in public order policing), a big, burly 'geezer' with a broken nose. The six officers under him were two white men that he'd brought in from TSG, and then four of us female officers – all white of course, apart from me. We were a small team working closely together, so it was important that we had a good dynamic because we would need to have each other's backs in a different way.

I started on juvenile protection: runaways, prostitutes, and what we used to call rent boys. Working in the West End meant I was often on night duty again. After eighteen months of normal office hours it came as something of a shock. I was back to patrolling on foot, but unlike those early days on teams I was always with another officer. Walking the streets was the best way of getting to know them, and the people who populated them. It was completely different working on these streets at night from visiting them as a tourist, or partygoer.

Runaways were surprisingly easy to recognize. Firstly because the Soho streets were no place for a child at two or three in the morning. Another clue was that the child who was otherwise grubby happened to be wearing a £100 pair of brand-new trainers. The worry then was that they were being groomed – adults earning their trust with expensive gifts in the hope of exploiting them into prostitution. If we saw children like this, we'd stop and start a conversation with them. If they were with a group of others, or adults, we'd try and get them alone, find out more about them. They often gave us false names, and this would become obvious when my colleague spoke to their friends who gave a completely different name. It was tough work, and their stories were often hard to stomach. Once we'd established their real names and rung them through on our radios, more often than not they turned out to be on the Missing Persons' Register.

It was good that we had located them, but sometimes the stories of why they had run away from home were harrowing. I remember one girl who we got back to the station, getting her warm and giving her something to eat and drink. As we waited for social services to arrive she told us that she had run away from home because she was being sexually abused by her mother's partner. We wrote up reports and passed them on to her local police force where, of course, we had no jurisdiction. This meant that after she left our custody we would have no idea what happened to her, whether she was forced to return or her allegations were taken seriously; there was no way of following up with her local force. We could be potentially taking her from one dangerous scenario and sending her back to another. It felt sometimes that we were just putting a plaster over things, but the wound remained – it wouldn't be long before a girl like that would run away again.

The West End was exciting compared to the areas where I had worked before – the lights, the people, the buzz. You felt as if you were in the middle of all the action, walking Soho on a Friday or Saturday night, seeing life in all its various shapes and sizes. Yes, there was a sleazy side to Soho – that is what it is famous for – but there was glitz and glamour too. Sometimes I was posted with one of my colleagues in an unmarked police car and we'd drive round and round the London streets, our area stretching all the way up through Marylebone to Paddington station. From behind the wheel of that patrol car we witnessed both the richest and the poorest parts of the capital.

What surprised me at first was how, if we pulled up at lights in Westbourne Avenue, a prostitute would jump into the back of the car.

'Is it my turn now?' she said.

I spun round in my seat, wondering what was going on.

'Hello, Mike,' she said, and then, pointing at me, 'Is this one new?'

The girls knew that it was our job to get them off the streets, and sometimes, rather than wait to get picked up and have an evening's business interrupted, they'd just volunteer themselves to be taken into the station early in the night. They had an understanding with the unit that if they'd been picked up once in an evening they wouldn't get picked up again.

'That's not how we do it, we need to have the evidence first,' I said.

'Oh, don't worry, love,' the prostitute said, 'you'll get used to how it works.'

I found this 'understanding' they had with the unit difficult. It didn't sit well with me, as I was used to doing things by the book.

Other times in my first few weeks I'd arrest them for soliciting but before I'd even finished cautioning them they'd have put themselves in the back of the car.

'Oh fuck off, we know how it works,' they'd say.

'Excuse me, I haven't even finished—'

'Let's just get to the station so I can get out again.'

We got to know some of the girls, and my biggest surprise was that they weren't always the types of women I had imagined – just like their customers weren't the types of men I'd imagined. I remember one married couple, who lived outside London. He would bring her in to work and wait for her while she picked up men. Her husband was effectively her pimp, and their children went to private schools on the proceeds. He would justify their actions by insisting: 'What's the difference between her going to a club, meeting someone and going back to his house? At least this way she's making money.'

Part of the remit of the job in Clubs and Vice was the decoy work that I had been trained for at Hendon. I loved the range and variety of the work and the rush I got from completing a successful sting. On a Friday or Saturday night, I would go into work as normal, but instead of changing into my uniform as I did when at Leman Street, now I would put on my make-up, let down my hair and dress up for an evening in jeans or smart trousers and a nice top. Our job was to go out in pairs to clubs in Soho, following up on intelligence we had received that licensing laws were being broken – for example, alcohol being sold to underage customers – or drugs were being dealt on the premises. It was important that these were clubs we would never go to as civilians, because we were pretending to be ordinary members of the public. We had to earn the trust of those who worked there by showing up week in, week out. So to do this work we would have to sign a form stating that we would not go to any West End club in our private lives. This would prevent us being compromised. Not everyone would agree to this caveat so they didn't want to do the work, but it didn't matter to me. I wouldn't ordinarily be going to clubs on a weekend, so doing this kind of undercover work gave me an insight into a world I would never have known otherwise. It was a stark contrast to how I spent weekends at home.

Each Saturday, Mum and I had the same routine. We would go to the market in Dalston High Street where Mum would examine the mangoes, complaining that they weren't a patch on the ones she had eaten as a girl growing up in Pakistan. We would pause at different stalls, picking the best from every bunch.

'This is how you know they're ripe,' she would say, showing me how to press the flesh to find the perfect fruit.

We would continue, plastic bags threatening to spill, to Sainsbury's and Tesco to buy meat and then head back home to fill the cupboards with chaat masala, cardamom and caraway seeds.

Like any good Pakistani daughter, in the house I was expected to wait on my brothers, guests and neighbours who would be regaled with stories of my mother's pride in my career, though vitally missing the detail of what I *actually* did. I made sure to offer her sanitized reports of desk work and coffee breaks because the truth would have kept her up at night.

But on one occasion we had friends visit from India who were so entranced with the idea of a British police officer that Mum insisted I go upstairs and put on my uniform to show them, and in turn they posed for a photograph beside me. There is one faded picture of Mum and me from that collection that I cherish, her in her shalwar kameez, me standing beside her in the uniform I would never ordinarily wear at home. I felt so awkward sitting there in the full get-up in my living room drinking tea, but it made Mum happy.

At that time, unbeknown to me, Mum and my little sister, Zinnia, had registered me with a rishta wali – a woman in a local clothes shop who kept a register of families who were looking to organize marriages for their children and who was known to find good matches. Zinnia had also registered me with shaadi.com, and both offered to manage my account for me – for a fee of course. Because of this it wasn't unusual at that time to come home from work and find Mum had opened the front room – our best room – to strangers keen to appraise a new potential daughter-in-law.

'Oh Mum, no,' I would say, moaning, 'I've just come home from work, I'm exhausted.'

But she would gently chide me, convincing me to put in an appearance, knowing that this man and his mother would be assessing whether I was marriage material as I put down glass dishes containing slices of bright yellow fruit and pistachios.

'Oh Mum, he's awful!' I'd whisper to her in the kitchen.

'Just come and speak to him,' she would try to persuade me. 'He's nice, with a good family.'

Mostly I'd refuse to go and sit with them and she'd just have to find a way to politely let them know. But on the rare occasions I agreed to serve tea and answer their questions, I would sit in the room opposite a nosy woman and her quivering son, him usually looking down at the carpet and appearing as awkward as I felt.

'What job do you do?' his mother asked me.

I shot a glance at Mum, who nodded, smiling.

'I work in the public sector,' I replied.

'She works for the police,' Mum said proudly, taking a sip of her tea and adjusting her scarf.

'How much money do you earn?' the mother asked me.

'How much does your son earn, aunty?' I replied, calling her 'aunty' to show respect.

From across the room I sensed Mum's discomfort and disapproval.

Decoy work was becoming more and more a part of my job in Clubs and Vice and I just couldn't imagine telling those people sitting in front of me that I'd spent last Friday night in a strip club paying a woman to lap dance just so me and my colleague didn't stick out among the rest of the clientele.

The mother got up and straightened her shalwar kameez.

'We don't want an independent girl,' she told my mother, and then, turning to her son, 'Let's go.'

Our small unit in the West End was also charged with setting up various decoy operations to target London's kerb-crawlers. Our operations were so successful that we would be contacted by police divisions all over London boroughs who had a problem with prostitution in their area. The first operation I was asked to take part in happened to be in my old borough of Tower Hamlets.

The strategy was pretty straightforward. Our male colleagues would wait in the unmarked van, listening in on the wires that were hidden under our clothing. Then I and my female colleagues would take turns to stand on a street corner, posing as prostitutes and waiting for a potential 'customer'. There were strict rules that we needed to follow to avoid entrapment. We weren't, for example, scantily dressed like some of the real working girls in that area. We also couldn't offer anything to men who stopped as that would be classed as entrapment; instead we were told to wait and see what they asked us for. They had to be the ones to suggest a sex act in return for payment to complete the offence.

My first day as a decoy prostitute was a strange one. It was winter and I was wearing jeans and a thick coat. I was grateful for the cold weather because it wouldn't come across as unusual to potential punters that I wasn't wearing anything provocative.

As instructed, I took my place on the street corner that we had picked out for the operation. It happened to be on a road that I had patrolled as a probationer, and I remembered how back then those working girls were more concerned for me walking alone than my colleagues ever were.

Now, to all intents and purposes, I was one of them.

I was wearing an open mic hidden inside my pocket so the officer in the van could listen to our live conversation. The van was parked about 100 yards up the road, far enough away not to draw attention, but also, I realized as I took up that lonely spot, far enough that they might not be able to make it immediately to my aid if something went wrong.

In that moment I was suddenly aware of the risks those women expose themselves to, day in, day out. In some ways, just like a police officer, they never knew who might be in that slowing car, but unlike us, they had no back-up. It suddenly felt like a very solitary role.

After standing anxiously for ten minutes, I saw one car drive past, the driver behind the windscreen taking a long, hard look at me. He drove around again, and again. My heart was pounding underneath my thick coat. He didn't come back for a fourth time.

I noticed there were a few Asian drivers who took a good look, and it was those I found hardest to look back at. It didn't occur to me at the time, but any one of them could have been someone who knew my family, or my mother, and just happened to be driving through east London at that moment. Perhaps if I'd given it more thought, I wouldn't have been standing there. Just like those shopkeepers who came out to have a look at a brown woman in uniform, this brown prostitute was worth looking at.

I stood and waited, sometimes walking round in circles just to keep moving, keep warm. Finally, a car pulled up and the driver rolled down his window.

'Are you working?' he asked.

I was aware of the entrapment laws, but technically I was working, just not in the way he thought.

'Yes,' I replied.

'What are you offering?' he said.

I remembered what I'd been told to reply.

'What do you want?'

'Well, what do you do?'

I knew my colleagues were in the van listening, I knew it was important that I got him on asking for exactly what he wanted. We stared at each other for a second.

'What do you want?' I asked again.

'What about . . .'

He said something I'd never heard of before, but it was clearly a slang term for oral sex.

I shook my head. 'No, sorry, I don't do that,' I said.

I looked inside the car. He was an older guy, his fat belly pressed up against the steering wheel. He looked me up and down from his driver's seat. His wedding ring glinted from the wheel.

'Well, what are you good at?' he asked. 'You can try what I want and see if you're good at it?'

I shook my head again. 'I don't do that.'

He sighed, muttering some expletive under his breath, and drove off. I quickly described the car to my colleagues through my wire, reading out the number plate, and at the end of the road I could just about see his brake lights going on as he was pulled over by a team in a car.

As nights like those wore on, I and my female colleagues would take turns to stand on the street and then warm up in the van in between. Bizarrely, it also became competitive between us.

'Did you see I'd only been out there five minutes and someone pulled up?' one of the girls said proudly when she got back in the van after her turn. In ten minutes she'd got three potential punters.

When it was my turn again, I was keenly aware of the fact that I could be standing there for thirty minutes in the pouring rain without any interest – after all, working girls don't go home when it rains. It was absurd that I became concerned over what my colleagues might say about my inability to attract kerb-crawlers.

The danger of posing as a decoy prostitute did not so much come from the men who were stopping to solicit my 'service' but from the women whose turf I was standing on. On one occasion I had been standing on a street corner for an hour or so and a woman came up to me. She was dressed in what people might imagine was the uniform of a working girl – a skirt slashed to her upper thigh, fishnet stockings and knee-high boots, and a low-slung top that revealed much of her cleavage.

It wasn't wholly unusual for an actual prostitute to come over to me while I was posing. We had scoped out the best places to base our operations, so we knew there were already girls working in the area – after all, that's why the men came here.

She came and stood next to me. I tried to ignore her and instead looked straight ahead, but she wasn't budging.

'Move,' was all she said, her voice low, laced with the authority of someone who was willing to stand her ground. And it clearly was her ground.

I didn't answer. I couldn't believe I was getting into a turf war with a prostitute.

'This is my patch, piss off,' she said.

'Oh really?' I replied, hoping my confidence would persuade her not to start anything. 'Well, I'm standing here.'

'You'd better move now,' she warned me, her voice tinged with threat.

I didn't move. Instead I wrapped my coat tighter around my body – my way of signalling to her that I wasn't going anywhere.

She moved closer to me until I could feel her against the sleeve of my coat. I could smell cigarettes on her breath.

'Move, get lost,' she said again.

I glanced surreptitiously at the van. I knew someone would be listening and all I could hope is that they had a way of dealing with this. I could hardly tell her why I was there, what I was doing. It would blow the entire operation. I was also worried she might have a pimp nearby watching. So I decided to try to intimidate her right back. I turned to face her and looked her dead in the eye without a word.

It was then that I saw a patrol car pull up just beside us. Two officers got out of the car, put on their helmets and walked towards us. The prostitute was still staring hard at me as if to say 'look what you've done now'.

The pair of uniformed officers split up, one of them taking me off to one side, another her. I didn't say anything, not while she was still in earshot – I had to keep up the act. But the working girl started kicking off so the officer who was standing with me had to go and help his colleague, and in the end they had to put her in the car and take her away. Before they did so, I was told to move on, so I walked a few steps away and then resumed my position as soon as the car was out of sight. I had no idea what those officers had been told or whether they knew I was a decoy or the real thing.

I went back to the van and sat inside to get a breather.

'All right?' one of my colleagues asked.

'That was a close one,' I said.

In this instance, my colleagues had been the ones who had called the local unit to come and move the prostitute on. Another time, it was one of the working girls themselves who called the police on me. She wanted me moved because I was on her patch and she didn't want any competition, so she reported me to the local unit. She told them that I was 'definitely new', that she hadn't seen me before but I looked 'too clean ... not like a druggy'. The local unit knew that we were carrying out an operation, but they still had to come and move me on so that the local prostitutes didn't get suspicious.

★

There's a pervasive idea of the type of men who use the services of prostitutes, but my stint standing on street corners taught me there is no such type. I had men pulling up to ask what 'services' I offered with children's car seats in the back, in Rolls-Royces and in minicabs; men in suits, young men, old men, white men, black men, Asian men. On one occasion a car pulled up beside me and the driver asked me how much. When I refused him he sped off and then stopped a few hundred yards away before reversing at high speed, his tyres screeching, all the way back to me, where he started shouting expletives. I was terrified and jumped out of the way of his car. But it has also been well documented over the years that police officers too have engaged the services of prostitutes – partaking in the very behaviour they are there to prevent.

In February 2022, a former police officer came forward and revealed to the IOPC how she witnessed a detective at Charing Cross Police Station having sex with a woman he had just arrested. She claimed that this was a regular occurrence and officers often used the toilets and cells at the station for sex with women who were highly intoxicated, regularly bringing prostitutes back to the station for this very reason. The woman, who only gave the name 'Sue' to protect her identity, recalled how the detective 'did not even flinch' when she opened the cubicle door and discovered him.

'It was a running joke that prostitutes knew the pin number to get into the cells better than the police officers,' she said. 'The security risk on that was appalling because the pin wouldn't be changed [that often] and this is a station where they take terrorist prisoners.'

Sue shared her experiences after the IOPC report which uncovered a culture of 'toxic masculinity' at the station. It is shocking to hear these stories because any amount of time in policing should teach any officer that these women who resort to selling their bodies are often doing it because they are vulnerable, poor or have been exploited. We get to know some of these women on a personal level, and they deserve our protection, certainly not our exploitation.

In January 2022, during a sting operation similar to the ones I carried out during my time in the West End, serving Met officer PC Tristan Downing was arrested for soliciting a sex worker. A misconduct hearing in July heard that he had continued working for four months after pleading guilty to the offence at Westminster Magistrates Court a month after the incident. The officer had received oral sex from a prostitute in his hire car, the act witnessed by plain-clothes detectives who later arrested him.

Downing, who was then working for North Central Command Unit, handed in his resignation in July 2022, though Deputy Commissioner Helen Ball, chair of the hearing, concluded that if he hadn't resigned, he would have been dismissed.

Following the officer's guilty plea, Camden and Islington's Commander Andy Carter said: 'We expect the highest standards of behaviour from our officers both on, and off, duty and this officer's actions fell way below these expectations. He was caught as a result of a proactive operation targeting those who exploit sex workers. The Met is committed to rooting out all officers who break the law or are involved in dishonest or disreputable behaviour.'

So why did they keep him on as a serving officer, albeit on restricted duties? They were still paying his wages even after he had admitted a criminal offence. How does an officer like that, or any other officer who has been caught soliciting prostitutes, carry out their duties if they are guilty of the same behaviour as the men they are arresting?

The issue here is the way that misconduct is dealt with in the Met, and that process needs to be completely overhauled. Baroness Casey's review found that on average the Met takes 400 days to finalize misconduct cases, which means that officers accused of the most concerning behaviours continued in their paid jobs for well over a year before they got an outcome. Not only that but 20 per cent of officers who faced a misconduct charge between 2013 and 2022 had been involved in two or more previous charges, and less than 1 per cent of them were dismissed. Baroness Casey also found that 'too often the organisation is reluctant and too cautious to define behaviour as gross misconduct, meaning it cannot dismiss many of those who fall short of standards of conduct the public would expect'.

However, black officers and staff were a searing 81 per cent more likely to have misconduct allegations brought against them and more likely to have the allegations upheld.

The misconduct process is not fit for purpose. It needs to be faster, more streamlined, with more power given to either the IOPC or an independent external body to carry out the investigation. A force cannot mark its own homework.

Tristan Downing received full pay for months even after he had admitted a criminal offence, and even more chillingly, Wayne Couzens was still receiving full pay while awaiting criminal proceedings for the murder of Sarah Everard. Why should the public be paying for officers who break the law?

Those types of decoy jobs were only a part of our work. Months down the line in this new role, the intelligence gathering we were doing in nightclubs was starting to pay off. I and my colleagues had been visiting the same clubs week after week, earning the trust of the barman and throwing away the shots he gifted us when his head was turned. I often got away with just ordering an orange juice, telling whoever was serving us that I was driving that night. It was an easy cover. If I did order an alcoholic drink, it was easy to lose it once we were moving around the club, putting it down, spilling it somewhere or flushing it down the toilet.

In one particular West End club we knew it was the landlord we needed an introduction to if we were going to be able to gather the intelligence we needed. We had heard that it was he who was dealing, we just needed to catch him in the act.

My colleague Suzanne and I had seen the landlord, Tony, around the club on the odd night, and we made sure he'd seen us chatting to his barman whom we'd befriended, so that, in his eyes, we were trusted regulars. On one night, Tony came behind the bar to serve. His barman introduced us and we sat chatting to them both as they worked.

'You girls up for a big night then?' Tony asked, passing us a couple of free drinks.

'Why? What you thinking?' Suzanne said, laughing.

Tony reached into his pocket and produced a tiny plastic bag with a little bit of white powder inside. 'Here, have this on me,' he said. 'Go and powder your nose, ladies.'

We waved the drugs away.

'I can't, I'm driving tonight,' I said, sadly.

'And I've got to work tomorrow,' Suzanne lied.

'Shame,' Tony said. 'Another time.'

We nodded enthusiastically.

We left that night feeling confident, the offer of a freebie having confirmed our intelligence. Now it was just a matter of getting him to offer to sell drugs to us. It wasn't enough to just have him in possession of drugs.

A week or two later we returned to the same club. This time Tony came out again to serve behind the bar, and the conversation turned to drugs very quickly. After all, he trusted us now.

'Come out the back with me,' he said, smiling.

We followed him through a maze of doors, leaving the bass of the nightclub thumping behind us. In his office, he locked the door behind us, and Suzanne and I looked at each other wondering what might happen next. He poured us both drinks. I took mine, wondering how I would lose it in that small office. I could hardly say I was driving tonight when, as far as he was concerned, we were there to buy drugs off him. I noticed there was a plant in the corner, so I went over and pretended to take a look at it, tipping bits of drink into the soil each time Tony turned his back.

He opened a drawer in his desk, and I mentally noted which one for the report we would write up later. From it he took a fat bag filled with white powder. Cocaine. There was a lot there: he was obviously showing off, trying to impress us. He opened one of the bags and tapped a little of the powder on to the desk. He took a card from his desk, rolled up a note and took some of the drugs himself. Then he leant back on his chair, closed his eyes and offered some to us.

'Go on,' he said, indicating the powder, 'help yourself.'

I looked at my colleague, wondering what excuse we were going to make. We had already taken him up on his offer to go back to his office to see what drugs he had, so how were we going to get out of having some here?

I could tell Tony was drunk and high so it wasn't too difficult to distract him. We kept him talking, hoping he hadn't yet noticed that we hadn't taken any of the drugs.

After a while, he had some more himself and then offered it again to us.

'Oh, we've just scored,' Suzanne lied, refusing his offer.

'Suit yourself,' he said, 'but take some for later.'

He took a small bag from his desk filled with the same white powder.

Suzanne and I looked at each other. We had evidence that he was dealing drugs – it had become blindingly obvious that Tony was supplying the drugs to the bartender, who in turn was selling to punters – now we just needed to figure out how to get out and back to the station. Tony was so drunk, he didn't seem to notice how keen we were to leave.

'We'll see you next week,' we said, unlocking the door and leaving him to his cocaine.

In reality we would never see Tony again.

We wound our way back through the streets of revellers towards Charing Cross Police Station. With those drugs in our pocket, we were now technically in possession of Class A drugs – which is, of course, a criminal offence. We needed to get back to the station and gain retrospective authority to be involved in criminal activity as part of our intelligence gathering – in other words, we needed to gain permission to possess those drugs.

Back at the station this was not the end of our night, but the beginning of a huge amount of paperwork. It's a less than glamorous way to end an undercover operation, but at least we had done it. We had managed to earn the trust of the landlord, and get the intelligence we needed. We wrote up our notes knowing they would be passed on to a different team who would conduct the raid.

The club was raided the following weekend, with us in it.

'Everybody stop! Stay where you are, don't move!' an officer shouted.

We stopped stock-still, shooting a horrified look at each other.

One by one the officers went round everyone in the club, taking our details too and searching us before they allowed us to leave.

Tony was arrested, and the club was closed down. Once it went to court, Tony received a prison sentence, and it turned out that he was connected to a much larger supply chain than we had realized. Detectives were able to take the whole chain down as a result of our work. Suzanne and I both received commendations.

I returned from another early turn shift one day to find Mum once again entertaining in our best room, which could only mean one thing.

'Someone has come to meet you,' my sister whispered, greeting me at the front door.

I was so tired. I'd been working hard on another decoy operation. I slipped off my shoes and winced at the blisters on my toes.

'Who's here?' I asked Zinnia.

'It's not Christian Bale,' she said.

I rolled my eyes.

I went into the living room with a tray of tea. Mum introduced me, and I clocked his mother looking me up and down.

Only when I glanced over at the man in question, sitting on Mum's best sofa wearing a smart pair of trousers and a blue shirt, did I notice that he refused to meet my eye. He seemed nervous too, and I noticed his leg start to twitch, tapping at the floor. At first I thought that it was because he might be shy, so I placed the tea tray on the table and sat down next to Mum who smiled at me as if to say 'this is a good one'.

It was his mother who started speaking first, asking me questions about my job as usual. I tried my best not to give away too many details.

'And what are your ambitions?' she asked.

I glanced again at her son, who was still staring at the floor. His mother and mine continued talking, and finally he looked up and met my eye for the first time. Then I saw it, a glimmer of recognition that passed between us. As my mum passed the biscuits, I tried to think where I knew him from, and then it came to me: I knew him from one of the kerb-crawling operations.

My own recognition must have registered on my face, because suddenly he started tapping his mother's leg as if he was a little boy, not a man searching for marriage. Not long after that they made their excuses and left.

'How strange,' Mum said afterwards as we cleared up the tea things.

'Yes, that was strange,' I said, smiling to myself.

5

Islington

Islington Police Station is situated in Tolpuddle Street in London's N1. The street gets its unusual name from the case of the Tolpuddle Martyrs, a group of six agricultural workers from the village of Tolpuddle in Dorset who were at the centre of one of the most notorious uprisings of nineteenth-century England. The station itself is a brick-built building designed to replicate Georgian style. It was completed in 1992 and so was relatively new when I arrived towards the end of the nineties.

I arrived at Islington in my first sergeant's role. I had first applied to be promoted after my success at running the pilot Domestic Violence Unit, but my sergeant had told me that I was not ready for promotion and my colleagues at Leman Street had laughed when I'd told them I wanted to be considered for one.

Back then, the way to move through the ranks was first to approach your immediate line manager – so, for an officer, that would mean approaching a sergeant – who needed to approve and back your application and vouch for the examples you were giving as your reasons for being able to progress through the ranks. It was an unfair system that meant one person was the gatekeeper to your promotion prospects, though it would be much later in my career that I would start to feel the real injustice of it.

I tried again in Clubs and Vice, and this time my line manager supported it (after the commendation I had received I don't know how they could have refused). As part of my written application I had to prove that I was a 'fully rounded officer' and had enough 'competencies' in various areas to become a sergeant, meaning examples of the work I had done leading teams or operations. Once I'd passed that part of the written application, I was invited to attend an assessment centre at the Empress State Building in west London where I would also take part in various assessments to demonstrate my ability to lead or organize. All officers go to the Empress State Building for their promotion interviews. There, several rooms are set up with role-play scenarios with actors and assessors present. Each candidate has to go into the rooms in turn – six or seven in total – and deal with whatever scenario is presented to them. It's nerve-racking because you never know what awaits you behind the door; you just have to go in, deal with it as best you can, and hope you did so proficiently. After the role play there is an interview, and if you pass all these stages of promotion you have to wait for a suitable posting. I did well in each of my scenarios, scoring in the top 2 per cent in each. That was how I ended up at Islington.

I went on to a team in Holloway where I was not only the only brown sergeant, but also the only female one too. Across the team there were four sergeants in total, all of them men and all of them white apart from me. Even the officers were all white, apart from one young Greek male on my team.

There was, however, a female inspector (the role above sergeant; each unit had their own inspector), but I quickly got the sense that neither the sergeants nor the officers rated her. She seemed pleasant enough to me, kept herself to herself, and left us to get on with our operational duties. That was one of the criticisms about her – just how hands off she was. But it seemed to me from witnessing the way that others spoke about her that the real problem was their own misogyny. Once again I came to the grim realization that I would need to work twice as hard as any man to prove myself on that team – and probably three times as hard as any white man.

This was the first time that I had found myself in a superior rank to some of my male colleagues, and it was a shock, clearly for them as much as for me. I noticed immediately that if I gave instructions to the officers – particularly the male ones – they would double check what I had said with one of the other sergeants before acting on my commands. Sometimes it was subtle: a glance to my male counterpart and a slight nod from him. Sometimes it was blatantly obvious: going to him for instructions instead of me.

I remember turning up at a stabbing and quickly taking control of the crime scene, giving orders to the officers, asking them about the CCTV, or who the witnesses were, and making sure that cordons were in place (when I got the sergeant's rank I'd asked one of my superiors for a piece of advice, and he'd said, 'When you arrive at a crime scene, no matter if the cordons are already in place, just move them back slightly to establish your authority there'). But when one of the male sergeants arrived on the scene the officers rushed to report to him, disregarding my orders completely.

Most of the time I could let it go, but sometimes when officers asked a male sergeant for orders despite just receiving them from me, I'd say, 'Sorry, was I just speaking in Punjabi then without realizing?'

I noticed too that when I was at the station with one of my white, male counterparts and any of the officers came in for advice, it was him that they went to first. I know my peers noticed it too.

'Have you noticed how the officers come to you and not me?' I said.

'It's just because we've been here a long time,' they replied.

By this point I had been in policing for a decade and had handled all manner of emergency situations and covert operations. It was clear that experience was not the issue.

As a woman in policing it is not only harder to get heard, but harder to give orders. The biggest problem I faced was giving orders to the older male officers. These were the guys who had applied for their sergeant promotion and failed. I knew there was a growing feeling among them that I had been promoted 'because I was a woman' or 'because I was Asian'. They didn't want to accept that I had earned my promotion and decided instead that it had been handed to me.

I heard whispers around Islington that because I had come from Clubs and Vice I knew nothing about frontline policing. I got wind that judgements were being made about my operational experience, that I wasn't a 'street cop'. Strange though it was, the officers would be the ones who would decide whether I was any good. It didn't make sense that I was having to prove myself again but that's how it worked and continues to work. Women are not only being watched from the top, but also by those beneath them in rank.

It was a big leap for me stepping into my first role as a sergeant. It was not necessarily the role that was challenging, but being a woman of colour in this role.

Baroness Casey's review pointed out that 'structurally women remain under represented in all supervisory and management roles' despite the fact that, until 2022, the Met had a female commissioner in Cressida Dick, and two out of the four assistant commissioner positions were held by women. While the last decade saw the number of female chief superintendents double and the number of female detective superintendents triple, women still make up less than a third of officers in all ranks above constable.

When you look at women of colour, the figures dip even further. 'Proportions of black, Asian and ethnic minority women are also highest in the lower and detective ranks,' Baroness Casey remarked in her review. 'But they make up a very small proportion of the workforce overall: 7% of detective constables, 4% of constables and only 2–3% at inspector and chief inspector ranks.'

Moreover, it's only certain women who make it up to the higher ranks, and it's not the working class or women of colour.

With so few women at a similar level to me, I had no one to turn to and learn from. In turn, officers weren't used to having to take orders from a female. And I know I wasn't alone. Baroness Casey noted that 'women, especially women of colour, need to work harder than their male counterparts at senior level', and her report included anonymous case studies of women who felt exactly the same as me.

And this isn't just a problem within the Met; women face problems commanding respect in leadership roles universally. The Reykjavik Index for Leadership measures perceptions of equality for men and for women in leadership. The target is a score of 100, which would indicate that societally women and men are equally suited for leadership – in other words, that there is a total absence of gender-based prejudice – but in their 2020–21 report the average index score for G7 countries was just 73.

A study in 2019 published by the *Personality and Social Psychology Bulletin* suggested that women in positions of authority were met with more resistance by men who perceived them as a threat to their masculinity. The study found that if women adopted a more 'collaborative or administrative' style of leadership, as opposed to authoritative, they faced less backlash from men in the workplace. This was certainly reflected in what I saw at every station I worked in. Female officers were fine if they were making the tea and doing the admin, but when it came to handing out orders, it was very clear who the men were prepared to listen to.

In her conclusion on women in the Met, Baroness Casey wrote:

> The Met is rightly proud of their previous Commissioner being a woman, and having women at the very top of the organisation, but women remain under-represented at all ranks in the Met above Constable. A 'boys' club' culture continues to play out across the organisation. The testimony and the data make it clear that mistreatment of women is a feature of that culture, which demonstrates sexism and misogyny.
>
> Across the organisation, there are also people who are challenging the status quo. But corporately, the Met needs to take misogyny and sexism, and the mistreatment of women that arises from those prejudices, more seriously.

If this pervasive culture of misogyny and sexism didn't exist at every level of the Met, I don't think that men, or even some women, would find it so difficult to take orders from a woman. As it stands, misogyny is so rife that still there are men and women in the Met who don't believe that women should be in positions of authority. They say that they respect the rank, but they also need to respect the woman who holds it. That has to start from entry level upwards, but we also need to lead by example. Those at the very top tend to lose perspective: they don't have visibility on what is going on around them, or what attitudes are filtering down from the old guard to PCs on the beat. It has to go both ways.

Back then, the sergeant role was split into two. We had a month of working on teams out in the patrol car, and then a month of working in custody and being based at the station.

The custody suite at Islington Police Station is located in the basement, and the custody sergeant's job is to process every prisoner being brought in. To do this job you need a thorough understanding of the Police and Criminal Evidence Act, and other legislation, policy and procedure. When officers or detectives brought in prisoners, it was my job to assess whether I had enough evidence to authorize their detention so that they could be interviewed. During these assessments it wasn't uncommon to be verbally abused, or threatened. Once I was even spat on.

Once people are detained it is the custody sergeant who is responsible for the welfare of that prisoner. One time doing my rounds, I was checking on a prisoner who had been arrested for a violent crime involving a serious assault. I was looking in each cell through the wicket, the small window in the door, and I noticed that one of the prisoners was lying face down on the floor. I opened the cell, found the prisoner unconscious, and called an ambulance. As you only have twenty-four hours to detain someone, the clock must be stopped while the prisoner is taken to hospital; all that paperwork must be processed and be beyond scrutiny because lawyers will find any reason they can to get their clients released. There was a real buzz working in the custody suite, dealing with prisoners and lawyers, and it gave the sergeant role great variety. You got to see your team in a different way – the types of prisoners they were bringing in, the kind of evidence they had to do so.

When I was on teams, I wasn't the type of sergeant

who was stuck behind a desk. I would arrive at calls alongside my officers and I wasn't afraid of arresting people. It was exciting to be at crime scenes because I loved the unpredictable nature of policing.

However, within a few weeks of my arrival at Islington, I earned myself a nickname among my colleagues – and at least this time it wasn't as bad as Nidgit.

I was filling up my patrol car at the petrol station one day when a call came through on my radio. I finished filling, paid and left, only I hadn't even made it off the forecourt before the car made a strange chugging sound and then stopped altogether. I radioed in for assistance, aware that the whole team would be listening in to my communication with the CAD room.

'You haven't put diesel in it instead of petrol, have you?' one of the male officers said.

'How do I . . .' And then it sank in. That was exactly what I'd done. Sitting there in the driver's seat, I put my head in my hands.

'Don't worry, sarge, we'll get the AA out to you.'

I'm sure I heard some sniggering on the other end of the radio.

After that my nickname was 'Diesel'.

Working as a decoy in Clubs and Vice had given me a taste for undercover work, and so while I was at Islington I applied to do the National Undercover Training and Assessment Course to add another skill to my professional CV. The course took place at Hendon and was an eight-week residential.

Part of the application for the course required building a criminal cover story that would be picked apart by the panel interviewing me, so it needed to be 100 per cent sound. This, in itself, called for lots of research. I didn't know anything about firearms, or knives, and my knowledge of drugs was limited to the decoy work I'd done at Charing Cross. I decided that my specialist area would be cloning credit cards. To build my back story, which I knew would be thoroughly tested at Hendon, I needed to learn everything about how criminals operated in this area, right from how you even clone a card in the first place. The story I fabricated was that I worked with an accomplice in a petrol station, and as people paid for their fuel, we copied the details from their cards. The key is to keep your personal details as close to the truth as possible; that way you can speak confidently and there is less chance of slipping up. I also needed a cover story for where I was from, because if you're building a rapport with a criminal, they might ask if you know this pub, or that shop or café, or this place. I knew south London well enough through friends, so it made sense to say I was from there. I could describe the streets, the shortcuts, the shops, the bars and restaurants where my fictional self would go socializing at night, and the cafés where my alter ego would have breakfast the next morning. I built a footprint in that area, and I got to know it inside out.

The process to be selected to be trained for undercover work was a complicated one. First, I was interviewed as my criminal character by the panel of senior undercover officers and HR, who pulled apart my story, looking for holes, quizzing me about the technicalities of cloning cards and asking me questions about new technology I'd never heard of – and that they'd possibly invented just to trip me up. A variety of fictional scenarios were thrown at me so they could see how I would react to them and how I would deal with them. I was meeting with a criminal and staying overnight; I had to sleep in the same bed with another undercover officer I'd never met before.

'How are you going to deal with that?' the panel asked.

'I wouldn't do it,' I said at first.

'You have to, you'll blow the entire sting if you don't.'

I wondered for a moment if they would ask the same of male interviewees – and whether their response would be as prudish.

'I'd sleep on the floor,' I said, finally. 'They could have the bed.'

There is no right answer, each person does things differently, they're just trying to learn if you can think on your feet, assess how you react to awkward questions, see if they can get under your skin.

We also had to do psychometric testing to get a place on the course. This was a multiple choice online test. The advice given was to pick the first answer that came into your head. The results would be analysed by a psychologist and would be followed by an interview with two further psychologists. If you passed the course and became an undercover operative then part of the accreditation requirement was that you had to see a psychologist three times a year to see how you were coping with the undercover work and assess whether you were under any undue stress in your personal life that might affect the job. If you didn't make those appointments, your undercover status would be classified as dormant.

The eight-week course was gruelling. It was strange being back at Hendon for a residential course. I hadn't slept there since I was a trainee. From my bedroom window I'd watch the recruits marching in their smart new uniforms and think of Cherry and myself at the back of the lines, swapping glances and giggling when the instructors weren't looking. So much had changed for me since then – I was returning to Hendon as a sergeant for a start – but when I looked at the cohorts that were here now, I realized not much had changed at all. I hoped I was representative of a more diverse Met Police but they were still mostly male and mostly white. Little had been done to improve diversity in the years I'd been out in the force.

The hours at Hendon were long, the work was hard and we were tested not only physically but mentally. We would start classes at 8 a.m., a mix of classroom work and lectures, playing out various scenarios or observing other members of our cohort doing theirs. We worked into the night writing up our notes, or learning how to debrief accurately, and then suddenly, just as we were ready to turn in for the evening, our instructors would surprise us with another scenario: 'You have to go to this bar in the East End and meet this person who is a drug dealer.' We would trek across London with perhaps only the name of the bar and a description of the man we were meeting – who would of course be another undercover officer within the Metropolitan Police – and later, these same people would return to Hendon to give us feedback.

These men (and they were mostly men) had some of the biggest egos I had encountered in policing – they were loud, full of themselves, and had an inflated sense of their own importance. If the area car driver thought he was God, I can't imagine what these men considered themselves to be. There weren't many female undercover officers that I met, though the ones I did bump into had often had to morph themselves into men to get to where they wanted to be. I remember one particular undercover officer who had a reputation for hating women. She could make life very difficult for females because she didn't want more women working in her specialist area – or perhaps because she felt that alienating women would make her 'one of the guys'.

After meeting a subject at a pub on the other side of London, we'd need to trek all the way back to Hendon to write up our notes, often finishing at 4 a.m. Then the following morning we'd need to be back at our desks by 8 a.m., ready for the day ahead. The instructors were getting us used to the unpredictability of this very specialized area of policing. In their world, events – and people – can turn on a penny, and you have to be ready to react. It was imperative that you could think on your feet and talk yourself out of any problems because there wouldn't always be someone listening in on a wire to come and rescue you.

It was daunting, and not everyone made the cut. There were many times when we would be listening to a lecture and an instructor would come in and tap someone on the shoulder and lead them outside. These people never returned to class: they were the ones the instructors had decided just weren't up for the job. As we got further into the course things felt very tense, all of us waiting for that tap on the shoulder, all the while hoping it would never come.

There were only two females on that course – me and another woman called April – and twelve men at the start. April and I were very different. She was very feminine in her floral skirts and pretty blouses, compared to me in my tracksuit bottoms and zip-up tops.

Every Friday the instructors would give us feedback on our work that week. It was often after these meetings that some classmates packed their things at Hendon and returned to their stations, having been told they didn't have what it took to become an undercover officer. On my third week the instructor sat me down and went through my notes. He looked up at me and then leant forward in his chair, his elbows on his knees. I had a feeling I was about to be kicked off the course.

'Nusrit,' he said. 'Do you think you can be a bit more feminine?'

'Sorry?' I said. 'I don't know what you mean.'

'The boys and I want you to use your feminine charms a little more,' he said, leaning back in his chair. 'We don't really see that in you with your tracksuit tops zipped up to the neck.'

He gestured to my clothes.

'This is just what I wear,' I said, shrugging.

'How about a dress or something?' he suggested. 'Show a bit more flesh. You've got it there so use that charm to work your magic on people.'

By people, he meant men.

'We want you to come back next week,' he said, 'but think about how you dress, use what you've got. Try laughing a bit more. You're really intense and we just want you to relax. Dress differently, behave differently.'

The men there were the ones with the egos, the bravado – 'jack the lads', to use a cliché – so I knew what he was saying to me without saying it explicitly. They wanted me to flirt. That's how they thought I would get better results, by flirting with the subjects. In their minds, women could only get results by using, as he put it, their 'feminine charms'.

'Be a bit more like April,' he continued, settling on an example he knew I would understand. 'I know there's a woman inside you.'

I really liked April, quite posh and fond of those sweet but sexy floral dresses which were not my style at all. She was a great girl, but I was nothing like her, and didn't want to start comparing myself to other women. I had never changed who I was to fit in and I wasn't going to start now.

'I like you,' he added, 'and I want you to use your feminine charms a little more.'

'It's just what I wear,' I responded with a shrug.

I knew one of the rules of undercover work was not to try to be someone you're not, otherwise you risk getting caught out.

Then he said, 'Maybe you and I could go out for a drink some time?'

I was shocked. I began to wonder if this wasn't just another test to see how I would react.

I didn't reply. I just looked at him.

The meeting ended, and I went home for the weekend feeling deflated, wondering if I wanted to go back or not. I spoke to Nina and we talked it through. We accepted that I would be disappointed to leave the course just because of his sexism, or the fact he'd made a pass at me. So I did return, I did try to relax more, to have a joke, to smile more, as instructed. It didn't mean that I was going to become what they wanted me to be or go and join the rest of them in the campus bar after classes, but I did what I had to do to stay on the course.

Once in the middle of a lecture, one of the instructors came in and passed a mobile phone to me.

'There's someone on the line who wants to speak with you,' he said. 'Find out what they want.'

'Me?' I asked, but he was already passing me the phone. 'Er, hello?'

The eyes of the entire class were on me.

The person on the other end of the phone was already speaking, really fast, telling me that the meeting had been arranged, quickly giving me an address and a time for it. I picked up a pencil, wrote a couple of words down.

'Can you repeat that?' I asked.

But the phone had already gone dead.

The class looked at me, as did the instructors.

'So, where are you meeting?' the instructor asked.

'He was speaking so fast, I didn't catch what he said.'

I heard the class sighing behind me.

'But in real life you won't be able to ring them back and say "Sorry, what did you say?"'

I felt my cheeks burn.

He turned to address the rest of the class. 'You've got one chance, one phone call, it might be the only one you get. So listen, keep them talking, get everything you need, write it down.' He paused. 'Pay attention.'

Another time, we observed another colleague's scenario. Ben was a funny guy. Usually silly, he always made the rest of the class laugh, but even he seemed afraid when he was immediately set upon by two instructors. They were angry when they came into the room, accusing him of grassing them up.

Ben tried stalling for time, to figure out what was going on. 'What are you talking about, man?' he said.

'When we got nicked the other day,' one said, 'how come we didn't see you getting nicked too?'

Ben quickly thought on his feet: 'Nah man, I ran.'

'What?'

'Yeah, when I saw the Feds coming, I just split, man. What? You think I'm gonna let myself get caught like that? Nah, man.'

The class laughed because we saw what Ben was doing – using his usual charm to talk himself out of a sticky situation. The key to undercover work is not to act as someone else, but use those parts of your personality that are likeable, charming. We were told that criminals do business with you if they like you.

Week after week, I stayed, I learnt. I passed more scenarios, I listened to the instructors' feedback, grew better at thinking on my feet. On one occasion, a colleague and I were sent to meet two undercover officers at a bar in central London to acquire a gun. We were given our brief to do a firearms deal. It was almost impossible in those scenarios to tell an undercover officer from the criminal he was impersonating. These people were arrogant, they weren't friendly, they asked loads of questions – technical questions about the type of gun you wanted, anything to catch you out. They made you feel as nervous as if you were sitting down with the Kray Twins themselves. Our role on that occasion was to make introductions to a second person. We were told this was often how we would work when it came to real undercover operations. One person would be the warm-up act and they would make an introduction to the next person, and the next, layering undercover officers with people who make them seem more legitimate. It also meant that when someone in the chain was inevitably arrested, it was harder to identify who had grassed them up. This is called creating theatre — an undercover term for making things seem realistic.

After eight weeks, I was told I had passed and now belonged to an 'elite club'. Our group of fourteen had dwindled to six people as so many hadn't made the cut. I was so proud of myself for succeeding where I'd witnessed so many fail, on what is widely considered one of the toughest courses in the Met. As a woman of colour I didn't know how it felt to belong to the Met, let alone any elite club. I bumped into an established undercover officer at work one day.

'Welcome on board, you're one of us now,' he said.

I understood what he meant: this was how the groups showed loyalty to one another, similar to the old boys' club. Being acknowledged in this way was an unfamiliar experience for me, but I was grateful for the extra respect my new status garnered me back in Islington.

For my first few jobs I was seconded from my day job to do some role plays for the undercover course, or just to play a silent 'girlfriend' to another officer to ease me gently into the role. Before every job we were read our instructions by a senior officer, and then we had to read them back to make sure we fully understood our duties. After that we signed paperwork confirming that everything had been agreed. There were strict legal and regulatory parameters around our work and what was expected of us, though I know it hasn't always been this way.

While I was at Islington I often had to wait for another undercover job to come along, and more often than not it felt as if the interesting roles were reserved for the men. I wondered when I would be able to put fully into practice everything that I had learnt.

Finally, a few months after I qualified, I got my first proper job. The Met had some intelligence that a minicab office in Hammersmith was a front for drug dealing. They needed to get an officer in to gain the trust of the people working there to see what exactly was going on. My job was to go and order a taxi from there. I was given a full briefing of what would happen next (I knew, for example, that I would be arrested but not where or when), but a lot of it would also involve playing along.

A few days later I arrived at the minicab office.

'Can I get a cab into the West End please?' I asked, leaning on the counter.

'Sure madam,' the man behind the counter said. 'There is a car outside for you now.'

We were perhaps a couple of miles down the road when suddenly I heard police sirens. An area car was behind us – I guessed it was for me. The minicab driver was forced to pull over.

'What the hell . . .' he said.

Before we knew what was happening, the cab was swarmed by officers, the back doors were pulled open and I was being dragged out. Even though I was a part of it, even though I had some idea of what was happening, I couldn't believe how realistic it was. This was proper theatre.

'Ow!' I cried, playing my part. 'What do you think you're doing?'

But those officers weren't messing around: they hauled me out of the car, spun me round, pushed me against the back of the cab and handcuffed me in plain sight of the driver who was watching agog from the driver's seat. I struggled against them, trying to do my part to make things seem realistic because we wanted the driver to see it all. Our hope was that he would go back to the cab office and tell them everything he had witnessed.

The officers started patting me down, searching me.

'I've got nothing on me,' I said. 'What do you think you're doing?'

But then one of the officers pulled from my pocket a plastic bag with some white powder inside. He held it up in full view of the cab driver.

'I am arresting you for possession of drugs,' a female officer said. 'You do not have to say anything, but it may harm your defence . . .'

I knew the script. I had read those lines out myself a thousand times.

They started walking me over to the area car, pushing me into the back, and as they did so I looked back at the driver who was still trying to see what was happening as another officer was talking to him. Finally we drove off, the show over.

'Are you OK?' the officer sitting next to me asked. 'We weren't too rough, were we?'

'I'm OK,' I replied. 'I've never been arrested before!'

'No, I suppose you haven't.'

We laughed.

'These handcuffs are a bit tight though, do you think you can . . . ?'

'Oh yes, of course, sorry.'

He loosened them a little, but we needed to keep up this charade until we got inside the station. Once there, the officer took off the handcuffs and I rubbed at the red marks on my wrists as we went over everything that had happened.

'Did you see the cabbie's face?' I said.

It had been a great piece of theatre, and it had been so exciting to take part in it. But that was just my piece. This was a set-up for the following day when my 'boyfriend' – or at least the undercover officer playing him – would go into the same cab office to apologize for what happened. In the confusion, of course, I hadn't managed to pay my fare and so the plan was that he would go there and do just that. Not only would he pay my fare, but he would give them more money by way of an apology, to earn their trust and in the hope of letting them see that we were one of them. First, though, we needed to give the cabbie time to get back to the office and tell them everything he had seen.

The operation was a success. The plan that we laid down worked perfectly and we managed to break the drug supply chain at that particular cab office. I felt proud of the part that I had played.

As the months went on, my undercover work became more interesting. At the time there was a huge number of cars being stolen to order and I was recruited to play the role of driver – the person who collects the car on behalf of the buyer. When a car is stolen, it is often laid down in a residential street for a few days to see if it attracts any attention. Once it's clear, the person who has ordered it sends someone, in this case me, to collect it from that residential street. The issue is that in that kind of transaction, nobody trusts anyone. The person who stole the car doesn't trust the person who is buying it not to take the car without paying. The person buying the car doesn't trust the person who stole the car not to take the money and keep the car. So the buyer and the thief will stand at a location nearby, and once they see that the driver has taken possession of the car, the money will be exchanged. But there is another problem: sometimes, even once the money has been exchanged, the car can often be carjacked, stolen back by the thief – the scam being that they get the money *and* the car too. This is why this particular role was especially dangerous.

I had been warned about this before I went to pick the car up. The advice I was given was not to stop anywhere after I had driven it away and to stay vigilant until I set it down at the agreed meeting point where another part of the team would collect the car.

On the day in question, I went as instructed to the residential street where I had been told I would find the car. It was a luxury car, a brand-new 4×4 BMW, so new in fact that I didn't need a key to get in (criminals who steal them from people's drives are able to copy the key fob through their computer systems). I'd been told exactly which route to drive out of the street, so that my fellow undercover officer, 'the buyer', and the subject would see me drive by in it and then exchange the money.

I was wearing jeans and a baseball cap, my long hair drawn back in a ponytail. I didn't want to attract any attention. I needed to get into the car as if it was my own and then start it up and get on the road as quickly as possible.

I climbed inside the car and sat behind the wheel. It was very luxurious, all cream leather interior. That was my first job done, now I needed to get on the road.

I'd never driven a 4×4 BMW before so I fastened my seatbelt and then looked at the controls. But something looked unusual, different. Within seconds it dawned on me: this was an automatic car. I'd never driven an automatic before. The gearstick wasn't anything like the type I was used to – it had letters on it, not numbers. I looked up and around me, saw a couple of people passing by on the street. I would arouse suspicion if I sat here too long.

Just at that moment my phone rang.

'Hello?'

'Everything OK? What's going on?'

It was my fellow undercover officer.

'Er, yes,' I said. 'No problem.'

I was too embarrassed to tell him I hadn't driven an automatic before. The only thing they had asked when they had recruited me for this job was whether I could drive.

'OK, well, we're waiting for you,' he said, hanging up.

I was aware that I was leaving him in a difficult position. The longer he stood there with our subject the more chance there was of something going wrong.

I can do this, I told myself.

I pressed a few buttons, moved the gearstick around, put my foot down on one of the pedals and somehow felt something release. I heard the purr of the engine and sighed with relief. I had no idea how I'd done it, but now I needed to work out the gear. I checked my mirrors and realized that while I'd been trying to start the thing, someone had pulled up tight behind me. It was now going to be impossible to get this huge car out of this tight spot.

I took a guess, moved the gearstick into D, that must

be 'drive', and felt the wheels move slightly. I quickly put my foot on the brake to stop it. Suddenly I was aware of a man standing beside my driver's window.

'Do you need some help with that, darling?'

I cringed internally.

'No, it's OK,' I said. 'I'm fine, thanks.'

He shrugged, and thankfully walked on.

I tried again, the car inched forward, but I needed to move it back to get out of this tight spot. I glanced at the gearstick again and moved it into R; this must be 'reverse'. The gears grated, attracting more attention from passers-by. Another man tapped on my window.

'Want me to do that for you, love?' he asked.

I shook my head quickly. The last thing I needed was a member of the public unwittingly handling stolen goods.

'I'm fine, thanks,' I mimed through the window.

But he didn't move, instead he just stood there. I felt the pressure even more, my palms now sweaty on the steering wheel. Another man joined him, and a woman with a pram who couldn't get by.

'Back a bit . . . bit more . . . you've got a bit more room, love, that's right . . . there you go.'

I followed his instructions through my mirrors, too stressed now not to be grateful for a bit of help but utterly embarrassed that I was attracting so much attention.

'Now turn the wheel the other way,' he continued. 'That's right, forward now . . . you've got enough room at the front . . . go on.'

I was aware of my colleague still standing a few streets away as I manoeuvred back and forth and then, finally, the front end was out and I was on the road. I waved a quick, mortified thanks and then I was off, heading through the streets as instructed. I passed the point where I knew my colleague was waiting and caught a glimpse of the man standing on the opposite corner to him – the subject. The money would be exchanged now and it was even more important that I just kept driving.

Within twenty minutes I was out of the tight north London streets – or at least they felt like that in that huge car. I'd been checking my mirrors constantly for anyone following, my hands gripping the steering wheel. I had to stay vigilant.

The plan was to drop it off at a retail car park just off the M25, and I pulled in where we had arranged, only as I did so I saw a car behind me, its indicator flashing, following me into the car park. I pulled into an empty space and saw the car do the same just behind me. Was I about to get car-jacked?

I was just about to stop when I suddenly had a bad feeling about the people who were following me. So I set off again, turning out of the retail park and back on to the motorway. I pulled up at the next service station and called in to let them know where I was. I then left the car and waited for my lift back. I could finally breathe again. It was done. Both me and the car were safe.

Afterwards I was taken back to a hotel for the debrief.

'What happened?' my colleague asked. 'You were ages bringing that car round.'

'You asked me if I drove, you didn't ask me if I could drive automatics. I was too embarrassed to tell you!'

He told me that rather than growing suspicious, the subject had been impressed that he'd recruited an Asian female driver. 'He called me a genius. He said no one would expect an Asian woman to be picking up a nicked car – he wants you on his team.'

We laughed.

The sting was successful, and those involved were apprehended, all of them receiving hefty prison sentences.

It had been a great role, but I was frustrated that all the others I was getting were sideline 'girlfriend' roles. I went to see the detective inspector of the undercover unit in the SO10 office at New Scotland Yard and voiced my frustration that women weren't being given better roles.

'I think that women should have the same opportunities in undercover work as men,' I explained.

He didn't say anything as I talked, just listened, and then when I paused, asked: 'Are you finished?'

'Well, no,' I said.

'Yes you are,' he said. 'There's the door.' And he pointed towards it.

I sat there for a few minutes, gobsmacked, while he totally ignored me. He hadn't been willing to engage with me. After being completely shut down by him, I wondered if that would be the end of my career in undercover work, but my complaint was simply ignored. I never heard anything about it again.

6

Heathrow Airport

In 2004, the Metropolitan Police rebranded the previously named Special Branch as the new Counter Terrorism Command (CTC), known internally as SO15. The origins of the branch date back to the late nineteenth century when it was based at Scotland Yard and made up of just twelve detectives. Today, CTC has increased to more than 1,500 officers, and its various departments are responsible for keeping London – and, by extension, the country – safe from terrorist activities and attacks on British soil.

The unit first came to my attention when I was still at Islington. They were looking for a sergeant to join their ranks. Joining CTC would be a new challenge for me. I knew that it was notoriously hard to get into, that the entrance exam itself was nigh on impossible, but I also knew that the work they were doing was interesting and exciting. From what I'd seen over the years, the people who worked inside Special Branch were eccentric and secretive, and those who could speak different languages were particularly welcome. As I could speak both Punjabi and Urdu I decided to apply, my ethnicity an asset for the first time.

The exam itself was strange. It wasn't just policing knowledge you needed, not even knowledge of London, or Britain. Applicants were expected to have a good understanding of every country in the world. I had to swot up on random things like flags and currencies. I would also need to have a good knowledge of their political systems, their current presidents and prime ministers, and their conflicts, past and present. Revising for the exam took months but I was determined that I would make it into CTC.

The day I arrived at Hendon to take the exam, I was surprised to see one of my fellow sergeants from Islington there. Neither of us had mentioned that we were applying beforehand, and perhaps that was for the best as it turned out that neither of us passed the exam.

Undeterred, six months later I decided to apply again (although my colleague was much more secretive about whether he was going to or not – it turned out that he did, and he failed again). For the exam I was tasked with writing an essay on the destabilization of the Middle East, and this time I must have got my flags right because I passed.

My first posting was to head up a team at Heathrow Airport, an hour and a half's commute each way from my home in east London, but nonetheless I was delighted. We were based inside an office at Terminal Four. Our job was to liaise with security services and to stop people they flagged as of interest and question them about where they were coming from, or where they were going and who they were staying with.

My team consisted of five older white men, all of them coming to the ends of their careers and most of them former protection officers – or 'prot' officers as they were known to us. Some of them had done fascinating work over the years. One had been Margaret Thatcher's personal protection officer and had been with her the night of the Brighton bombing; others had provided security for royalty or prime ministers, and all of them had travelled the world with Special Branch. If it was at all strange to them to have a female boss, and an Asian one at that, they didn't show it. These men had earned their stripes. They were not insecure or filled with arrogance and ego like some of the men I had worked with before, so they were very happy to work with me, and vice versa.

Each day it was our job to go between terminals stopping people of interest as they entered the country. We were able to detain them under Schedule Eight of the Terrorism Act, interview them, search their baggage and even download the contents of their phones. This was an exercise in intelligence gathering, a case of layering up intelligence for the security services to give them more of an insight into where these people went and who they associated with when they got there. Everything we gathered from our interviews was written up and sent to the intelligence services.

From behind the controls at immigration, we saw the whole world arriving and leaving through London's doors. We even saw some celebrities too: Kylie Minogue, Liz Hurley, Katie Price, an Arabian prince. In contrast to my work at all those various stations within London, suddenly our capital city felt tiny compared with Heathrow Airport. In plain clothes we could mingle with holidaymakers in each terminal, though sadly we couldn't buy duty free. We didn't have much contact with airport staff, or even the armed police there as they were supplied by the local station. Our job was simply intelligence gathering.

It was 2004, and in the long aftermath of 9/11 security was at its tightest. Passengers could no longer travel with liquids and queues for the X-ray machines snaked back and forth endlessly. The people we stopped believed that it was a random check, though it rarely was. As soon as they checked in with immigration officers, their passports would be flagged up and then we would step forward, take them out of the queue and ask them to accompany us to an interview room.

'Could you please come with me?'

'Why?'

'Oh, we just need to speak to you about something.'

They never argued though. They were either on their way somewhere or eager to get back so they were always willing to comply with whatever we asked of them. Sometimes, just the data from the download on their phones was enough for security services. Other times, if we had flights arriving from countries of interest, we would all go down to the terminal and wait behind the immigration controls. Those times our checks would be entirely random. Everyone has seen it before: people pulled from a queue and asked a few questions about where they've travelled from, where they're going.

It was exciting work, and we knew we were just one

link in the chain, just one cog in the wheel that was working for a safer country. We might never know the full details of who the people we were apprehending were or who they were connected to – though we might know perhaps that they had links to terrorist groups such as Hezbollah; we stopped one of them once travelling to Turkey – but we knew we were doing important work to keep the country safe in unsettled times.

I was also still being called for undercover work during this time, and the jobs were getting increasingly interesting as my experience developed and I was assigned more complex work.

Ben, my colleague from the original course at Hendon, was on a long-term project to infiltrate a drug-smuggling gang up in the north-west of England. I was contacted because they needed someone to play his girlfriend to give him a legitimate back story. So each weekend I would get on a train and head up north where I stayed in his house. Again, I was read my instructions, briefed on what my mission was in relation to intelligence gathering. My role was not only to provide legitimacy for Ben, but also to get to know the other people in the gang, and find out what they knew.

Working with Ben was great. We already knew each other well from the course and had always got on so it wasn't hard to banter with him for the benefit of the people he was associating with. On weekends we would go out for dinner with these people, sometimes as a foursome with their wives too. My job was just to be myself, to charm them into thinking I was one of them. I remembered one of the wives was a nail technician so I'd chat to her about her business, compliment her on her nails. It wasn't just about getting information out of people, it was about building friendships. Sometimes I liked these people. Sometimes they were nice. But I had to remind myself they were also criminals, and I was a police officer.

Ben and I spent every weekend together for six months. We went out for drinks, to clubs, shopping to the supermarket. It was important that we were seen doing normal couple things. We also invited other undercover officers up for the weekend, or for nights out, playing our friends. Every part of the job was about creating theatre.

Sometimes we had great nights out with the people we met — once we even went to a boxing match with them — but when the front door closed at the end of the night, we went off to separate rooms where we wrote our notes and debriefed. It was ultimately a dangerous job. We were mixing with high-profile criminals who, if they became aware of our real identities, could cause us serious harm.

At this time during my career I was also applying for my inspector promotion. I had been a sergeant for a number of years by now and was ready to move up the ranks once more. To complicate things, I was also being offered a job as Ben's 'full-time' girlfriend, working permanently in infiltration rather than just at the weekends. I was told the job could continue for a year, or even two. The only thing was that it would compromise my plans for promotion: I wouldn't be able to start the promotion procedures until my re-entry to the force. As much as I liked the thought of this full-time work as an undercover officer, I wanted to progress within the Met so I turned it down.

★

Over the last few years, infiltration work has become a very contentious subject. In June 2023, a public inquiry found that undercover police operations in the 1970s and 1980s to infiltrate left-wing political groups were unjustified and should have been closed down. These 'spycops' have given undercover officers a bad name, for we now know they were gathering intelligence on people who posed no threat to the country. These were officers who were left unchecked, rogue in communities, and many of them went on to have relationships with women and even father children within the communities they were infiltrating well into the twenty-first century. These women did not know that they were sleeping with undercover police officers. They were effectively providing the 'theatre' that should have been the job of fellow officers – just like I had done with Ben. How could they have consented to sexual relationships with men who were not revealing their true identities, who were only using them to provide cover for the job?

The report, by Sir John Mitting, did not focus on the relationship element of undercover policing. However, it did criticize the 'striking and extensive' amount of information that officers gathered about political activists which therefore deprived them of their right to a private and family life. He concluded that those activists posed no threat to public order.

This type of infiltration is very different from the undercover work that I and my colleagues did. We were going into scenarios where crimes were taking place; we were infiltrating drug rings, or arms deals, not public order offences. The people who were being infiltrated in this scenario were simply groups with a specific political view. They were being surveilled without good reason.

The instructions all undercover officers are given is that our work must not intrude upon Article Eight of the Human Rights Act – the right to privacy, including someone's family life, their home and their correspondence. For example, in the course of the work that I did undercover, I never went to someone's home. If we met it would be in public. Our own contracts were very clear about that.

The spycops inquiry was set up in 2014 after a stream of revelations surfaced about the misconduct of undercover officers. Some of them, we have since learnt, were spying on the family of Stephen Lawrence, the black teenager murdered in south London in 1993. And then of course there were the men who infiltrated green activism and commenced relationships with women who had connections to these groups and who could therefore unwittingly provide a cover for these men. Mitting said that sexual relationships between spies and women became commonplace and were 'a perennial feature of the SDS (Special Demonstration Squad) throughout the remainder of its history'.

As far as I know, these officers only filed their reports once annually, did not undergo the sort of psychometric testing we were required to, and did not meet with psychologists three times a year to be assessed as fit for the job. After each undercover job that I did, I was required to write up my notes and debrief straight afterwards. I had to work within a regulatory and legal framework. That was not the case with these officers, 139 of whom between 1968 and 2010 were sent on deployments that often lasted four years and in that time spied on more than a thousand people. You've got to have regulation and a framework because if you don't you will end up in the situation that SDS did. My parameters were clear, I knew exactly what I was doing in each job, but people left without parameters will go rogue. Psychologically they were left to their own devices; they were effectively managing themselves and the lines became blurred because they weren't accountable to anybody.

They also stole the identities of dead children to bolster their own back stories, which is of course unforgiveable. But what is most shocking is that the report concluded that the SDS had operated under orders from the Home Office, and that their reports were passed on to MI5.

Details like these are not familiar to me because of the strict code of conduct that was impressed on me and my colleagues by the time we were doing undercover work from the early 2000s. We were told categorically never to form intimate relationships with those we were monitoring, so I can understand why the British public, and particularly those who were the victims of these spycops, were angry and hurt by their actions. Commander Jon Savell of the Met Police stated: 'We know that enormous distress has been caused, and I want to take this opportunity to reiterate the apologies made to women deceived by officers into sexual relationships, to the families of deceased children whose identities were used by officers, and to those who suffered a miscarriage of justice because of the actions of SDS officers.'

These men should never have been left alone. I believe that they were abandoned by the departments that deployed them and so their idea of fact and fiction blurred. In any undercover situation you are always a police officer first and foremost. It takes skill and courage to go into potentially precarious situations with dangerous people. These attributes were not present in the type of work these officers were doing.

Back at Heathrow, we were on high alert. On 7 July 2005, terrorists detonated devices on three different underground trains and one bus in central London. Fifty-two lives were lost and hundreds of other people were injured. It was an horrific attack, and one that I narrowly missed myself as each morning I caught the Piccadilly Line all the way across London to Heathrow Airport. If I hadn't left so early I could have been one of thousands of commuters who were caught up in the bombings.

After the incident, airport security tightened even more. We worked longer hours, stopped more planes, extended our searches and increased the number of countries that we kept an eye on. At that point, flights to and from Doha, the capital of Qatar, as well as Turkey were particularly being monitored so we were doing random checks in the queues and gathering intelligence for security services. In the days and weeks after the bombing, the atmosphere shifted. The buzz of holidaymakers was replaced with a tense silence as flyers second-guessed other passengers and security alike.

But because of my ongoing undercover work, there was real variety to my day-to-day work. Between the security role at Heathrow and criminal activities, I was constantly kept on my toes – though I was beginning to see that so much time and effort could be put into operations that didn't yield a result, and that could be disappointing.

I had been drafted into an undercover role in an operation in west London where there had been a series of racial assaults in a park. I and one of my male Asian colleagues, Sanj, had been chosen to walk in and around the parks where the attacks had been reported. We had hoped – though that seems like a strange word to use in hindsight – that the attacker might try to target one of us. Local crime squad officers had been dotted around the park to leap to our rescue should that happen. Some of them I'd seen before, others had been drafted in from all over the Met – two men playing football were definitely part of the decoy operation; another woman and what appeared to be her boyfriend chatting on a bench were another. Sanj and I walked around, had an ice-cream, chatted for hours in the hope of making our stroll, our own piece of theatre, seem genuine. It seems odd now to think of us walking for hours, waiting to be attacked simply because of the colour of our skin. I kept alert but tried to relax and blend into my surroundings. We weren't wearing any wires for that particular operation, and we had no idea if the people who might attack us would have weapons, or where they might spring from. We were literally sitting targets. But apart from the usual – some shouts of 'Paki', which I had grown used to – there were no leads by the end of the day and we all went home without an arrest.

Another time the police had received several reports from young women of a physiotherapist operating out of a gym in south London who was performing lewd acts while massaging them. I had to come up with a cover story about an issue with my neck and book two appointments with him.

From the moment I stepped into his consulting room I had a bad feeling about him. He was a young guy, perhaps late twenties, stocky, beefy, clearly worked out a lot, but there was something about him that just felt creepy. I had been equipped with a bag that had a secret camera hidden within it, so I put it down on a chair, just as I'd been instructed to, so that it was facing his massage table. The physio made me lie down on my front while he took a look at my neck and back. From the reports police had received we were aware that women who had been asked to do this believed that he was masturbating as they lay on his couch. I braced myself, knowing that if this was the case at least the camera would catch it. I felt sick as he touched my neck. But I left both appointments with no evidence that that was what he was doing.

It could be disappointing leaving an operation with no intelligence, but in that scenario I was grateful that I hadn't become another of his victims. You walked an odd line doing undercover work. Sometimes working to make London a safer place meant putting yourself in certain situations that you wouldn't ordinarily consent to.

In the Met Police, promotions come up in seasons – windows where the opportunity to progress up the ranks become available, usually twice annually. I had first applied to be promoted to inspector during my time at Islington, though this was refused by the female inspector there who said that I wasn't 'fully rounded' – whatever that meant for her. This procedure was so subjective. Often it is dependent on how long it took your own manager to progress through the ranks. This outdated system meant that if you had a boss who didn't like you, or if your face didn't fit, or if you weren't one of the white men patting each other on the back down the pub, it was harder to make progress. I had done so well in my sergeant exams, coming out in the top 2 per cent, that the advice I'd received afterwards was not to wait too long to sit my inspector exams. But after my inspector at Islington refused to support my application there was little I could do to make progress, which felt frustrating and unfair.

But when the next season of promotions came up, I approached my inspector at Heathrow. Like the men on my team, he was an ex-protection officer, an old-school inspector near retirement without the sort of ego that might've prevented others from supporting me. He was based at Scotland Yard so we didn't have much contact day to day, but during one of our meetings he saw no problem in supporting my application to go for an inspector promotion.

Much of my tenure at Heathrow was spent putting together my application, writing up my competencies so that I could make it through to the next round – another visit to the assessment centre where, again, just like for my sergeant exams, I would be required to take part in various scenarios. I was thrilled when, thanks to my chief inspector supporting me, I got straight through to the assessment centre.

One of the scenarios at the assessment centre was being asked to deal with an underperforming officer and then writing up a development plan for how we could take things forward to get them to start performing. Another required me to brief a plan of action on how I would tackle a burglary problem in the area. I presented my plans to the panel, and they quizzed me on them, making sure they were thoroughly sound. Again, I passed with flying colours, scoring high in each scenario, and eventually received my promotion to inspector.

Altogether I spent eighteen months based at Heathrow Airport within SO15 and I really enjoyed the global outlook the role afforded me, but when a job was advertised internally for the London Prisons Unit, I decided to find out more. The unit was responsible for all of the London prisons within the M25 and collecting intelligence from the prisoners housed there. My job at Heathrow had given me a wider perspective, but now I felt it was time to turn my attention closer to home.

7

Scotland Yard

The London Prisons Unit was located at that time on the sixteenth floor of the iconic Scotland Yard building near St James's Park. Like Wall Street has become synonymous with New York's financial markets, Scotland Yard has become a shorthand to represent London – and, by extension, British – policing. But the Met's history with its headquarters has been a long one. When Robert Peel first founded the Metropolitan Police in 1829, the headquarters was a private house in Whitehall Place which backed on to a street called Great Scotland Yard. Towards the end of the century the headquarters expanded, moving into various premises around the original site and further into Great Scotland Yard. But in 1967 the headquarters moved again into a specially constructed site on the Victoria Embankment, called Scotland Yard as a nod to its humble beginnings. This was the building I stood in front of on a breezy day in 2006.

The London Prisons Unit was responsible for every prison within the M25, including all of the most notorious ones like Belmarsh, Wormwood Scrubs, Pentonville and Brixton. The unit was part of the Met Police's SO15 Counter Terrorism Command, and mostly responsible for gathering intelligence from prisoners by applying for surveillance powers to monitor prison visits and phone calls. It did this by way of a team of prison liaison officers who were based in the prisons and had good relationships with prison guards who got to know the prisoners and their habits. Terrorist prisoners were often housed with regular crime prisoners, so it was good to understand how people communicated, who their visitors were, what they talked about, how their habits changed, and if those changes should concern us. In the giant melting pot that is a prison, housing everyone from terrorists to violent criminals, it is always useful to have eyes and ears because, after all, it is in such institutions that networking can and will take place.

The inspector I was to work under was – surprise – another one of the old-school white male officers who were more akin to army captains. He was at least a nice, decent man, pleasant enough but waiting for his retirement to come round like a lot of senior officers within the Met.

My work at Heathrow meant that I had experience of working with intelligence agencies and had a good overview of how gathering intelligence worked globally, and of the intricate web of activities terrorists would weave. It also meant that I was quickly able to grasp how our approach within the London Prisons Unit could be improved. Early on, I noticed that many of the terrorist prisoners (who we called TACT prisoners after the Terrorism Act), behind bars for crimes such as fundraising for terrorist organizations, were being held in Category B prisons, yet all of our intelligence-gathering resources were being pumped into Category A prisons like Belmarsh.

'We have no visibility on the people who are getting lesser sentences,' I wrote in an email to my inspector and the superintendent.

I realized that the same went for immigration detention centres. We had no visibility there and therefore no idea who they were housing or whether they might be a danger to our citizens. I knew that security services were watching people who arrived or left the country at official checkpoints, I'd done it myself, but what about those who made it across the border by other means? Who was monitoring them? Who was checking who their visitors were and whether they were people of interest to us?

The superintendent liked my ideas and asked me to come up with a plan for how we could implement more intelligence gathering.

'I don't want to be stepping on my inspector's toes,' I said to him.

'No, that's what we absolutely want you to do,' he said. 'It keeps him on his toes too. You carry on.'

The superintendent listened to me, often complimenting me on my ability to tackle difficult situations and difficult people. I was progressing well, and for the first time in my career I thought that this must be what it is like for the average white man to proceed through the ranks, to be supported, encouraged, praised for his work. I had received recognition before, but I'd often felt I had to fight to be noticed – but it didn't appear to be the case here. It felt like maybe my time had come at Scotland Yard.

Within months of me arriving at the London Prisons Unit we were able to expand, putting prison liaison officers into both Category B prisons and immigration centres. It was the job of those officers to build relationships with guards, to find out more about who these people were mixing with, and why, and soon we were receiving so much more intelligence than we had had previously.

During my first year at the London Prisons Unit I was still being called for undercover work. I still loved doing it, but as my workload increased, it became harder to take time out from the day job.

One of the jobs I took on was to go and meet a subject about acquiring guns. On occasion I would wear a niqab on undercover ops so as not to identify myself. After all, there weren't many other Asian female undercover officers (in fact at one point I was the only one in the whole country). This time, too, I donned a niqab, tucking the recording device – which was similar to a dictaphone – into my bra before going through my instructions with the superintendent, as always. I made my way across London and into one of the main train stations. It was a boiling hot day and underneath the niqab the sweat was pooling at the bottom of my spine. I was very aware of the recording device, knowing that it was running the whole time I was taking part in the operation.

I looked up at the station clock, peering out on the world from the small window that was afforded to me through the thick black material. My train was about to leave. I crossed the concourse quickly and descended a set of stairs towards the train that had just arrived at the platform. Only as I did so, I realized I couldn't run as fast as I usually could because of the niqab. It reached all the way down to my feet, which I could barely see as I looked down. As I descended the steps, the doors to the train opened and what felt like a thousand football fans emptied on to the platform, chanting and shouting. Some of them got out of the way as I hurried against the tide of them, some knocked into me as if I were invisible, while others shouted insults and threw beer at me.

'Go home,' one snarled.

I winced underneath the niqab, imagining the women who dress like this every day who are subjected to this kind of abuse.

I reached the train just as the doors closed and settled down in my seat for my journey to the north of England. I had agreed to meet with the subject in a public place. We had chosen a greasy spoon café some distance from the station. When I arrived a few hours later, I made my way to the place he had suggested. I was aware that a local surveillance team would be 'picking me up' – a police term for watching me to make sure I got to and from the rendezvous safely. To help them identify me we had arranged that I would carry a red handbag – though of course I wouldn't know who they were.

I arrived at the café and was able to identify the subject. He looked a bit surprised to be meeting with a woman, and especially confused to be meeting with a woman wearing a niqab, but was polite, and we sat down to discuss business.

As police officers we cannot act as 'agents provocateurs'. This means we must not incite or provoke a person into committing an offence. I was mostly there to listen, and I was lucky that this man said all the right things that would be picked up on my recording device.

I left after about half an hour and made my way back towards the station. As I did so, I stopped at some traffic lights, aware that the surveillance team would be watching me from somewhere. I stood with my red bag in front of me so I would be easy to spot. Only as I waited, two other women wearing niqabs came and stood next to me and, unbelievably, when I looked down, I saw that one of them had a red handbag too. How on earth would the surveillance team be able to follow me now? The traffic lights changed and all the pedestrians surged forward. All I could do was make my way back to the station and get my train back down south. My recording device would later be bagged up as evidence.

When I got back and got in touch with my cover officer, I was told that the surveillance team had indeed been thrown off course by the appearance of the other two women wearing niqabs. Apparently they had followed the wrong woman and it was only when they pulled up outside a primary school and saw that she was there to collect her children that they realized they had lost me. But the job had been successful, and the intelligence I gathered had helped them.

Perhaps it was because I had been so focused on the job that I didn't picked up on the office politics that was going on around me. I'd been in the prisons role for about a year when my inspector announced abruptly that he was leaving. I'd had no idea just how bad things had become between him and the superintendent, and when he explained to me in his office, I suddenly felt terrible as it dawned on me how they had used my energy and ambition against him. He had allowed me to run the office day to day, but with a creeping feeling I realized that where I thought I had been finally recognized for my abilities by the superintendent, I had actually just been a useful tool to force the inspector from his job for reasons I never found out. I felt like a pawn in their game.

'I'm sorry,' I said to him. 'I didn't know this was happening to you.'

'Don't be sorry,' he said, 'just watch your own back.'

I felt conflicted. I believed my inspector, and felt bad about everything he told me he had been through. How they had turned on him, favouring me, effectively making his role redundant. Most of my surprise came from the fact that my direct experience of the superintendent and other senior leaders had actually been positive up until this point.

His departure obviously also left an inspector role vacant, and as I had been running the department I felt pretty confident that I could apply for the position once it was advertised internally. I had arrived as a sergeant but had already passed the promotion process to inspector. I knew I'd have to fight to get the role, rather than be waved into it as I had seen happen to many men who had come before me, but it seemed like I was perfectly placed to step right in. Understandably, then, I was a bit surprised when I was told by my superintendent that they had somebody in mind for the role.

'This is somebody we know who has more experience,' he explained.

'But how can they have more experience when I've been running the unit?' I said.

He didn't have an answer for that, just told me that it had already been decided.

But it made no sense. What about due process? So often throughout my career I had watched other officers – members of the 'boys' club' – get retained by departments on a nod and a wink because the bosses had made it sound like their friend was the only one in the whole of the Met who could do the job. Those men (and they were men, and they were always white men) were not required to move around the Met to gain more experience or 'rounding' like me and my BAME colleagues. Some of them had been retained by the same command for the entirety of their career, moving through the ranks without receiving experiences in any other areas. What I was witnessing, right in front of my eyes, was structural failings and systemic racism and sexism. It would have made sense if they were going to advertise the job, but just waving in someone else they knew was so unfair.

'But what about the application process?' I asked.

I was aware that my questions were making the senior leadership team uncomfortable, and that it would be better for them if I just accepted what they'd told me. But I had worked hard for that department, I had implemented a lot of changes; how could they reward me by bringing in someone who knew less than me about how the unit was run? I knew that if a man had been doing my job it would have just been a formality to wave him into a permanent position. I wasn't even asking for that – I was just asking for the opportunity to apply for the role formally.

And so I was tenacious, I refused to give up. I made such a fuss that they were forced to go through an official application process, and I did finally get the job because I was the best candidate and not because I was their mate. They would remember this, though. My card had been marked.

The Counter Terrorism Command was then made up of various units. To name a few, there was the London Prisons Unit, the National Prisons Unit, and there was the Source Unit, a covert operations outfit responsible for recruiting people to feed us intelligence, perhaps more commonly thought of as recruiting informants.

The heads of the other units were all white and male, apart from my counterpart on the National Prisons Unit who was another Asian officer, Syed Hussain. Syed was tall, well spoken, dynamic and extremely knowledgeable about his department. Not much escaped Syed, yet I was still surprised by what he came and told me a year or so after I was made inspector. The Met Police's CTC had been invited out to Washington DC as guests of the FBI. The purpose of the trip would be to share our experience of encountering all forms of extremism and radicalization in our prisons, and to exchange good practice with our American colleagues to help improve our collective management of such prisoners. It was an important trip, and one that could be really useful to the department.

'Did you know about the trip to Washington DC?' Syed asked me one day after a meeting.

I shook my head.

He told me the names of the colleagues from the various units that made up CTC who were going. 'I've been invited at the last minute only because my inspector suddenly can't make it,' he explained. 'They offered it to someone else first and only me as a last resort.'

'So why haven't I been invited?' I asked.

Syed shrugged.

It turned out that aside from our meetings three times a week, there had also been separate planning meetings taking place between our other colleagues as they readied themselves for this trip to America.

'Does it seem a coincidence to you,' I asked Syed, 'that the only people not invited are the two Asian officers?'

Syed shook his head and sighed. 'Nothing surprises me, Madam,' he said – his nickname for me because I was a higher rank than him.

This was an amazing career opportunity, yet they had been keeping it secret from us, treating it as if it was a lads' trip abroad. I knew instinctively that I shouldn't raise it with my superintendent. I would be seen as causing a fuss, I'd be branded a troublemaker, and my card was already marked after making them go through that official recruitment process. But, as always, I couldn't help myself, because it simply wasn't fair that Syed and I had been left out. And if it wasn't for his inspector not being able to go neither of us would even have heard about it.

So in our meeting a few days later I asked my colleagues outright about the trip to Washington DC. 'Who's going?' I asked, putting them on the spot and watching them squirm in their seats as they gave me the names.

Word must have reached the superintendent that I now knew about the trip because within a few days the invitation was extended to me and Syed. I accepted without hesitation, and it turned out to be one of the highlights of my career.

A few weeks later, as Syed and I boarded the plane for Washington DC, we saw that our other colleagues were sitting elsewhere. I stared at my boarding pass thinking that there must be something wrong, particularly when we discovered that our seats were in business class.

'Can you have a look at this, Syed?' I asked him. 'We can't be sitting here.' I knew that officers were only allowed to travel economy so I assumed that there must be some mistake – or was it a test of our integrity? 'I'm not getting moved when they realize we've taken someone else's seats, it'll be really embarrassing,' I whispered to him.

'Madam,' he insisted, 'these are our seats.'

'But they can't be.'

I called the air hostess over to check our boarding passes.

'Yes ma'am, these are your seats,' she said.

'Just sit down, Nusrit,' Syed whispered, 'everyone is looking.'

I couldn't believe it – the American embassy where we got our visas from must have arranged this.

The trip itself was wonderful. We spent a week in Washington DC, touring the sights including the White House and the House of Representatives, and visiting FBI Headquarters where I gave a keynote address at a national conference about our intelligence gathering within the London Prisons Unit. We were also given a tour of the DC Central Detention Facility, the Bureau of Prisons and the Correctional Treatment Facility.

The way that we treat terrorist prisoners – or perhaps any prisoners – in the UK is very different from how they are treated in the United States, and I found that quite shocking. The sentences people receive over there can be 100, 200, 300 years, ones that will far outlive their human lives. They didn't need to monitor their terrorist prisoners because they did not allow them to have visitors, they did not allow them to make phone calls, or even really to mix with other crime prisoners. Even though it would have saved on so many resources if we treated our prisoners in the same way, it didn't seem to me that it was congruent with their human rights.

On one visit to a detention facility outside Washington we passed a sign that read 'You are entering Ku Klux Klan County' with a big Confederate flag. I quickly slipped down in my seat, terrified in case the car broke down and they saw Syed and me.

I pointed the sign out to Syed. 'Look,' I whispered.

'Yes, I've seen it,' he replied.

'Can you go any faster?' I asked the driver.

I had visions of us being surrounded by men wearing white sheets and pillowcases over their heads.

'It's no problem, ma'am,' he said, 'there's nothing to worry about.'

Each evening the FBI agents took us out for a meal and a show. It was incredible to think that Syed and I would have missed out on this if our colleagues had had their way.

Back on the London Prisons Unit, the changes I had made in terms of monitoring Category B prisoners and immigration centres were working well, only we soon realized that there was a difference between collecting a large *quantity* of intelligence and collecting higher *quality* intelligence. For example, some of the intelligence we received from our officers in prisons would focus on whether prisoners had grown facial hair, or whether they were praying more frequently than they had been doing, or perhaps even fasting. I would look at intel reports stating that someone had grown a 'Muslim beard' and ask, 'What exactly is that?'

It was clear that some of the prison liaison officers across the country had no idea about Islam, or the fact that it is common for people to turn to religion out of boredom, loneliness or even fear during their sentence. That didn't mean that they were becoming radicalized or extremist and it felt wrong to put them in the CTC database, which we shared with security services and which would seriously impact their lives, because of somebody's lack of understanding and ignorance. There were even a lot of cases of people converting to Islam in prison for better food or for more time out of their cells to pray. Yes, they might have been playing the system, but it didn't immediately signal that they were a threat.

'We need to do some training with our prison liaison officers,' I told my superintendent, 'because this type of intelligence is not good enough. We need to know what else they are doing to arouse suspicions. Growing a beard doesn't mean they are a fanatic.'

Syed and I worked closely on this, and training was set up by the National Prisons Unit to help liaison officers to understand signs of radicalization and how they weren't just looking for obvious displays of religion but a consistent change in behaviour or patterns. Many of the terrorist prisoners 'recruited' some of the prisoners who were inside for violent offences simply because they were fearless and they wanted protection. We needed to understand what was happening to those prisoners after they left prisons and who they were associating with in the outside world.

All three of the units connected to prison activity were under the supervision of the superintendent and one detective chief inspector. On my appointment to inspector, I had spoken to the DCI about wanting to go for promotion when the next round came up, so when he announced that he was being seconded to a different department for a few months and that another inspector would be stepping into the role of acting DCI in his absence, I was perplexed.

There were three inspectors including me who were all eligible for the position, but only two of us had indicated we wanted to go for promotion, so why had he handed it to his white male colleague with no due process?

I asked him, reminding him that I'd already mentioned that I was interested in applying for the promotion. He would know, after all, that a successful tenure in an acting role would help to round out my application. But instead of acknowledging the conversation we'd had about me wanting to progress through the ranks, he claimed he couldn't remember me ever mentioning it to him. By chance I had an email where I clearly stated that to him, and so I forwarded it, saying that I was disappointed that there had been no due process in appointing the acting DCI.

He was left with no choice then but to share the

opportunity among us. Apparently he apologized to the person who had been lined up for the acting role by saying I'd 'made a fuss'. Twenty years after I'd first joined the force and still my valid requests were viewed as 'fuss'. I knew it was viewed that I had taken the opportunity away from him, but my point was that it shouldn't have been gifted to him in the first place. We were both working in the same role and I had already registered my interest in a promotion with my superior both in person and via email. Yet again I found myself having to fight to get the same opportunity as my male white colleagues.

As it turned out, my few weeks as acting DCI were in name only. I wasn't given the chance to make any decisions, as my colleague had done before me, and staff still went to him for decision-making even though he was new in the department.

But I wasn't going to be deterred. When the next round of promotions came round the following year, I made clear my intention to apply and my DCI, who had by then returned, agreed to support my application. The promotion process was the same as it was for all ranks. First you write your application, describing your competencies and giving examples of the good work that you have done, and then you ask those who have worked with you as your superiors to verify this. I emailed all three of my superiors in turn, asking if they remembered the examples I was giving and asking whether they would be willing to verify my work to support my promotion. Each in turn wrote back saying they were great examples, and that they would absolutely verify them. Everything was heading in the right direction.

It was at this point in my career that I met Shabnam

Chaudhri. I had been aware of Shabnam within the organization mostly because we were a rarity – two women of colour in senior roles within the Met – but we had never met before. At that time, in 2010, Shabnam was a chief inspector and was running classes within the Met to help black, brown and female employees prepare their applications. First she would give us feedback on how strong our examples were (these examples would be graded by an independent verifier between one and five – five being the top mark), and second, she would quiz us on our examples to prepare us for a panel doing the same at the assessment centre. It's not unusual for senior officers to help other officers prepare for promotion in this way as not only does it help us progress, it also then helps with their own applications for promotion.

There were three of us in her class, all women, and Shabnam asked us to volunteer to read out some of the examples we had put down in our application. Everyone was silent, shuffling awkwardly in their seats. Classically, no one wanted to be the one who went first.

'Nusrit?' Shabnam gestured for me to begin.

I read out the example I had been working on in class, and when I finished, Shabnam said, 'Wow, that's a really strong example. Well done, Nusrit.'

As time was getting ever shorter, she invited me to visit her at her station in Shoreditch to do a mock testing panel so that she and one of her senior colleagues could scrutinize my examples in preparation for the real thing. It is not uncommon in the Met for people to put down examples that they were not directly involved in, which is why they need to be verified by a superior, and why panellists will quiz you about the details.

'We'll do it as a mock board,' she said.

I was grateful for any help I could get. This was the first time I had been supported like this. I was aware that the white boys and girls had their own groups where they helped each other, and I was just so grateful that Shabnam was willing to help me.

That day in her office, Shabnam and her colleague listened while I gave each of my examples, and then they quizzed me about precisely what my role had been in each of them, where I had made operational decisions, why hadn't I chosen to do X or Y, and what exactly had been successful about it.

'These are really strong examples,' Shabnam said afterwards, 'and you know them inside out. I'm impressed.'

She was absolutely confident that I would succeed in my application for promotion, and this bolstered my confidence.

Only days before the results were due out, my chief superintendent called me into the office and asked how I was feeling about them. I told him I was a little nervous.

'Well, don't worry if you haven't got through, it took me many attempts.'

It was a strange thing, not even to wish me luck with the results, but I assumed he was just offering me some advice. Although when the results were published, it turned out I hadn't got through. Had he known? I was stunned to find I was given the lowest score for many of my examples, and some of them hadn't even been marked. I had failed.

The next time I saw Shabnam, a week later, she asked, 'How did you do? You obviously got through.'

'I didn't even make it through the first stage,' I replied.

'What?'

'My senior colleagues refused to verify my examples.'

'What?'

It was true. When the verifier had contacted all three of the men I had put down as people who could corroborate the work, each one in turn refused to confirm that I had done it.

'But why would they do that?' Shabnam said. 'You had already asked them if they would be willing to support it.'

'They told the verifier that they couldn't remember me working on any of those incidents,' I explained. Because of that, the verifier had refused to mark it altogether. 'The verifier instead suggested that the panel needed to look at *my* integrity – they thought I must be lying.'

'But this is awful,' Shabnam said. 'They can't do that, that could affect your entire career.'

'I know.'

I felt utterly hopeless. I couldn't believe that my three senior colleagues in SO15 had done that to me. These were people I had worked with for years, people who had once been so impressed with me. Suddenly I heard the words of my former inspector ringing in my ears, warning me to watch my back. I knew that from their perspective I had been a pain. I had effectively forced them to include me on their white male trip to the United States and I had raised concerns that they had overlooked me for the acting chief inspector role with no due process, and this was my punishment. They were blocking my opportunity for promotion.

'We need to take this further, Nusrit,' Shabnam said.

I could see how genuinely shocked she was that this could have happened. She had witnessed how I had prepared and seen for herself how strong my examples were. She also knew that all of my senior leaders had already confirmed with me directly that they remembered me working on those jobs, and that they were happy to verify me.

'Do you have any proof that they said that to you?' Shabnam asked.

'Of course,' I said, 'I've got their emails. I followed the process.'

I knew by now that Shabnam was unafraid of speaking her mind. So with Shabnam's support, I appealed the decision, and also put in an official grievance against those three men in senior management. We enlisted the help of the Police Federation rep (this is the staff association for police constables, sergeants, inspectors and chief inspectors), but he seemed extremely nervous. Though he instructed us on what steps to take, he wouldn't put his name to it or speak up for me. He knew that taking on those men at that level was a very dangerous thing to do. They had already closed ranks once; taking them to task over their behaviour towards me was only going to irritate them more. But if they could do this to me, they would do it to others too.

Shabnam was incensed. She went to see Rose Fitzpatrick, who was then head of the Women's Network within the Met. It had been decided my appeal would be heard in SO15 which meant that once again they would mark their own homework, stick together and protect each other. I fiercely objected to this, but they insisted on it. When Rose heard what was going on and saw through our lens what was happening, she arranged for it to go to another command.

Accompanied by Shabnam, I arranged to see Commander Richard Walton who was head of SO15. I told him to his face what these three men had done, and also explained – as far as we could see it – why they had done that. It was because I had rocked the boat, because I had demanded that there should be due process when appointing senior roles. They just couldn't accept that a brown Muslim woman could be the same rank as them. I was not grateful enough, not respectful enough, not quite enough for them in any way.

All we could hope was that these people would see what was happening, but mine was not an isolated example.

In 2008, Tarique Ghaffur, then Britain's most senior Asian police officer, agreed an out-of-court settlement over his racial discrimination claim against the Metropolitan Police. Ghaffur was an assistant commissioner when he lodged a tribunal against the Met in 2007 accusing the then Commissioner of Police Sir Ian Blair of being racist. Ghaffur claimed that he had been sidelined, discriminated against and humiliated in his role as chief of security planning for the London 2012 Olympics. His complaint reached all the way to the top of government, with the then Home Secretary Jacqui Smith announcing an assessment of the treatment of ethnic minority officers in England and Wales. Boris Johnson, who was Mayor of London at the time, also launched an inquiry into alleged racism within the Met.

Ghaffur later accepted a last-minute £300,000 out-of-court settlement from the Met in exchange for withdrawing his claims against the organization. He also signed a gagging order preventing him from talking about what he had experienced during his career.

A few months prior to that, Sir Ian Blair had also faced accusations from another senior Asian officer, Commander Shabir Hussain, that he had been passed over for promotion because 'my face did not fit and did not fit because I am not white'. Hussain had accused Blair of having favourite white officers among his ranks who leapfrogged black and Asian officers for promotions. Hussain described them as 'the golden circle'.

A tribunal would eventually conclude in the Met's favour, but it is clear that the Met has a history of being accused of being racist and blocking the promotions of BAME staff. In 2020, a Freedom of Information request by the *Daily Mirror* revealed that twenty-four times more white police officers had been promoted than non-white colleagues in the three years previously. The request also showed that not one of the forty-three forces of England and Wales employed staff as ethnically diverse as the population it policed. 'The stats further show that of the 84 times officers were promoted into the most senior positions in the last three years, only one BAME person, recorded as being mixed race, was successful,' the newspaper reported. 'In total, 24 of 43 police forces in England and Wales have black officer numbers still in single digits. Only around seven per cent of all officers are from BAME backgrounds, of those four per cent are senior officers.'

The National Black Police Association told the newspaper: 'Despite an unprecedented number of initiatives – including setting targets for the percentage of BAME officers in forces, positive action programmes and direct entry – the impact on BAME representation in policing has been negligible.'

Baroness Casey's review in 2023 also noted what Ghaffur, Hussain and others have highlighted. The further you travel up the ranks, the less likely you are to encounter officers of colour:

> The higher the rank within the Met Police, the less representation from Black, Asian, and ethnic minority groups there is. Superintendents, Chief Inspectors, and Inspectors are the least diverse ranks (between seven per cent and ten per cent are Black, Asian or from other ethnic minorities, compared with 17 per cent of Constables). There are some exceptions. The proportion of Black, Asian and ethnic minority Chief Superintendents has grown from 4% to 12% over the last decade. In real terms however, this actually represented a cut of 35 Black, Asian and ethnic minority Chief Superintendents, due to an overall reduction in the number of Chief Superintendents in the Met.

The BAME officers within the Met who spoke with Baroness Casey also shared their experiences, with one senior officer telling her that someone had once asked at the opening of a large meeting, 'Did you get to where you got to because you are black?' Another person told the review: 'BAME officers are consistently overlooked for jobs and promotion. If a BAME officer is promoted it is openly discussed how they only got the job because of diversity and quotas. BAME staff are viewed with suspicion and seen as outsiders.'

She also noted a repeat pattern from both retired and

serving officers of colour of being blocked for promotion by their white superiors on the grounds of not having sufficient 'experience' (her quote marks, not mine). 'It took me eleven years to get promoted from Inspector to Chief Inspector, despite putting in countless applications to get promoted,' one senior officer told her. 'I was always told that I needed more experience in a specific area.'

Officers also reported that BAME staff were less likely than their white counterparts to get opportunities to 'act up' – stepping into their superior's role when they were away – or to temporarily fill a vacancy.

Thankfully my own appeal for promotion was upheld, though I was encouraged then to drop my grievance by my Police Federation rep and the head of SO15.

'What are you going to achieve, Nusrit? You've won your appeal and that's very rare, and you'll now go to the assessment centre along with everyone else. Why have this hanging over your head?'

I pushed my grievance against my senior colleagues, but the internal grievance team closed my case after I had won my appeal – they didn't seem concerned by the wider, blatant implications of white men blocking BAME people from promotions. I argued that they should be referred to the Directorate of Professional Standards. After all, if they could do it to me, they could do it to anybody. But they were not interested. Nobody wanted to deal with their integrity issues even though they had been more than happy to question mine. These men would go on to progress through the ranks to the very highest levels of the Met Police.

So I did finally get to the assessment stage, though later than everyone else. I remember, as I was waiting for my chance to go for my assessment, sitting round a lunch table with the senior leaders who tried to block me. Among us was an inspector who was waiting for the same thing, who I would describe as their golden boy. The superintendent and other superiors were patting him on the back, asking him how he was feeling about it all and promising him that he'd do well. No one said a word to me or asked how I was feeling.

I went to the assessment centre a few days after their golden boy. I came out as one of the top in the process, scoring all fives. And their golden boy? He failed and didn't get his promotion, despite all their backslapping and offers to help him through it.

Back at command, no one from the senior team asked whether I had passed or failed, though I did see them commiserating with their golden boy. It was almost as if they believed there had been an injustice, that I had – again – stolen an opportunity from one of their own. But what did it matter what they thought? I had officially earned my promotion. I was now a chief inspector.

A few days later, I was speaking to my counterpart on another unit over the office phone. I knew that he was friends with the chief superintendent who had blocked my promotion so I deliberately wanted to share my news with him.

At the end of our call I said, 'Oh, by the way, I was successful in my promotion.'

'Oh, well done, Nusrit,' he said, though I sensed the surprise in his voice.

In his haste to end our call he forgot to replace the

handset properly, so I sat at my desk and listened as he immediately made a call on his mobile.

'You'll never believe it,' he said, calling the chief super by name so I could instantly identify who he was talking to. 'The Doris got through. How did you let that happen?'

'Doris' is a slang term for a woman, a derogatory term – or at least that's how I had always heard men use it within the police. I couldn't believe what I was hearing, not only the words but the tone of them, the utter disgust that I, a brown woman, had got a promotion and one of their people hadn't.

Of course, I couldn't let it lie, so the next time I saw him a few days later I looked straight at him and said, 'Oh, by the way, I heard what you said on the phone, when you wondered how the Doris had got through.'

'What? Oh no, Nusrit, I didn't mean it like that . . .'

He coughed and spluttered, tried to backtrack, but there was no digging himself out of that hole. Unlike these white men, I'd had to fight for my right to apply for promotion, and then when I got there I had passed first time. But it still wasn't good enough for them, I still didn't deserve their praise or admiration. I saw then exactly what my first inspector had warned me about.

'Watch your back, Nusrit,' he had said, 'because they will turn on you.'

And he had been right.

I had received my promotion but I was yet to find a new role, so until I did I had to stay in the London Prisons Unit working for the people I had complained about, which made life really awkward. I was keen to leave, except for every role I saw advertised internally I was told there was already someone waiting in the wings for the position. It was the same old story I'd heard again and again. I and many others were passed up for new roles which then created a list of people who were stuck in their old rank, and far from coincidentally the people on the list were often black, brown and female.

I had already taken on several fights within the Met but it seemed that this would be another one. I complained to the head of HR Clare Davies about how unfair the current posting process was. I'd had enough of people choosing their mates for jobs, rather than people who had the right skill set. It obviously wasn't just me who had complained, as the Met agreed to review and restructure the posting process, which also meant – while the review took place – I was forced to stay in my unit surrounded by men who resented me for complaining about their behaviour.

Usually when someone has received both their promotion and their new posting, they get a date to start the new post, which gives the unit time to recruit someone new to replace them. But that didn't happen in my case. Instead, my superintendent decided to recruit a new inspector while I was still waiting to receive a posting – effectively making me redundant. Their reasoning was that they knew I would be leaving at some point and they couldn't afford to have the role unoccupied. They gave the role to someone else within SO15, again without due process – and it just happened to be another white man. I didn't know then it would take eighteen months for me to receive that posting.

Life on the unit started to feel really uncomfortable, not only for me but for my reports. They knew that this new guy was their boss in waiting, so they were no longer sure who they should be taking orders from. On more than one occasion a staff member came over to ask something and we both answered – even though, technically, it was still my unit.

The same happened when it came to meetings. The incoming inspector was shadowing me as I helped him to get to know the unit, but before long he was taking it upon himself to attend the meetings instead of me.

It was not only an utter waste of resources, but it really started to affect me. I felt undermined and embarrassed. It was like they were forcing me out. On a professional level it also started to feel childish, fighting over who was going to a meeting, or giving orders. I could have stepped aside and let him get on with it, which was obviously what my superiors wanted me to do, but I couldn't make myself redundant when I had no idea how much longer I would have to wait for a new posting. I knew that was the whole point of his arrival: it was a punishment for speaking out against my superiors – or at least it felt like that.

Eventually, though, after many months the friction between us became untenable. I went to see my superintendent.

'It's impacting on the rest of the team,' I said. 'There's no clear leadership and the staff need that.'

His suggestion was that I be seconded to another unit while I waited for my promotion. At the time the Met were launching what they called the Change Programme. This was being carried out to streamline or amalgamate different units in the hope of releasing more officers, sergeants and inspectors into borough (meaning frontline policing). The Met had realized that resources could be deployed more efficiently this way, and senior leaders were being seconded to work on the programme.

'I'll move you on to the Change Programme for your development,' he said.

Though I hated to give my superiors a sense of victory, it sounded like the ideal solution, plus it meant I would gain experience in another area.

When I saw a chief inspector role was available within Counter Terrorism Protective Security Command, it seemed to me the unit would be a good next move for me, especially with my background in counter terrorism. I had got to know the commander who was heading up the command, through my work with the Change Programme, so I approached him to see if this was something he would consider me for.

While I had been working on the Change Programme, the Met had undergone a change of its own in its job posting process. Now, instead of officers getting into jobs on a nudge and a wink from one of their mates, they needed to be put forward to a central postings panel, a body that would approve the move. This felt like huge progress and sounded much fairer than what I'd dealt with before. I hoped it would put an end to the nepotism that had been the prevailing way of recruiting within the Met.

But the commander wouldn't consider my application.

'Sorry, Nusrit,' he said, 'we've already got somebody in mind and he's got the qualities that we need for the role.'

'But I know the command,' I said, 'I've just been responsible for its restructure, I know it inside out.'

'But you've never worked in protective security,' he said.

And that was the end of the conversation.

Once again, despite the fact that outwardly the Met had reformed their postings panel, I could see that the old system still worked against new blood coming into departments. The commander would later state that he couldn't recall ever talking to me about any potential postings.

A few days later, I was in a meeting with Deputy Assistant Commissioner Neil Basu who was praising me for my work on the Change Programme. He knew that I was still awaiting a chief inspector posting. During our conversation, he asked me whether I had considered what my next move within the Met might be.

'Well, I was interested in the position that's available in the Protective Security Command,' I told him, 'but the commander has told me that they've already got someone lined up for that role.'

Neil didn't say anything in response, I didn't expect him to, but a couple of weeks later I bumped into the commander again and asked him if he had any other roles coming up within his command. He seemed irritated by my question, and was rather dismissive as he explained.

'Well, Neil Basu has told me that I've got to go to the postings panel and bid for you,' he said.

'Oh really?' I said. 'Why?'

'He said because you worked on the reconstruction of the command and he said you'd be good for it.'

I'd had no idea that he had put that particular flea in his ear, but secretly I was pleased someone was backing me for once.

DAC Basu was his superior so of course he had no choice but to obey his orders, but it seemed to me he was irritated that the person he had lined up wouldn't be getting the job after all. Begrudgingly, I was given my first permanent role as chief inspector within the CT Protective Security Command that I had restructured.

8

Lambeth Road

The building that occupies 109 Lambeth Road is not a particularly beautiful one. It is, in fact, entirely the opposite according to many – an imposing brutalist structure with huge concrete external stairs and a large concrete ventilation shaft which has almost become a monument in its own right.

The building is most famous for being home to the Met's Forensic Science Laboratory, also known as the brain stem of policing in Britain, and houses 600 forensic scientists inside, all working at the forefront of technology to help solve our most complex of crimes.

The building standing there today was built in the 1960s, but the original Edwardian construction that occupied 109 Lambeth Road also had a history of policing as it was the site of the first Public Carriage Office which regulated London's cabbies. By the time I arrived in 2015, it was known as Police Central Command and was home to various specialist units including the newly created Protective Security Command, and it was to be my new professional home.

My department within the Protective Security Command was the Threat Assessment Unit, responsible for the physical safety of the capital. That meant hardening targets, for example putting barriers on bridges so that cars could not slam into pedestrians. It was about making London safer from attack, so my work in counter terrorism was integral to the job. There were many different departments and units within the command that kept London safe. One, for example, entered public buildings like museums and galleries and tested their security. These plain-clothes officers were, to all intents and purposes, members of the public, and would cross the ropes, try to get into staff-only areas where no visitors were allowed, and push the security system to ensure that the public were as safe as possible from potential acts of terrorism.

Alongside that, the Threat Assessment Unit was working in silo, gathering intelligence and doing threat and risk assessments solely focused not on protecting the public but on the day-to-day protection of the royal family, Members of Parliament and foreign diplomats. The final unit that came under its remit was the Search Unit. These officers – known as PolSA (police search advisers) and often recognizable by their blue caps – were specially trained to carry out fingertip ground and river searches in areas where there had been serious and/or fatal crimes and incidents.

When I arrived on the unit there were three chief inspectors, and each of us had different portfolios. In charge of threat assessment, my team would produce reports each day after looking at all the intelligence gathered from our various security services and brief across the Met on crime and terrorist activity. I worked alongside a female inspector from Royalty and Specialist Protection, who would gather her intelligence from protection officers and local forces (for example, perhaps a member of the royal family had an event in the north of England and there were known anti-monarchists operating there), but it seemed to me early on that the whole Royalty and Specialist Protection unit would be a lot more efficient and streamlined if we shared all the information and threat data. It would also benefit all of the staff to work across both units, developing their professional practice and skills in all types of policing and intelligence gathering. There was resistance to this, of course. Specialist teams can suffer from elitism, tending to assume that no one else will understand their work, so they can often be quite closed off to the idea of sharing information. Some had worked in their unit for a long time so any change or movement was fought. I stopped and absorbed the whole dynamic, quietly confident I knew what needed to be done.

'We don't want an overview of everything,' the protection officers insisted, 'we only need to know about the threat to royalty and diplomats.'

But I was convinced it would benefit the whole command and the Met if we had a cross-sharing of information and resources and if everyone had an overview of each other's work.

Luckily my inspector, my direct subordinate, agreed with me, and so we started to implement the plan.

My new role as chief inspector meant that I was less

involved in the day-to-day operational work and more of my time was taken up with staffing and management issues. That meant I no longer had time to do undercover work, which had in any case been drying up as I'd moved up the ranks in the force. It was disappointing but I understood that the higher you go up the ranks, the more you need to be based in your unit. It was a trade-off to progress in my career.

The changes that I implemented were going well in terms of intelligence sharing, and the quality of that intelligence was improving, so I'd only been there about six months when I was given responsibility for the Search Unit too – the specialist team that carried out fingertip searches at serious crime scenes. I welcomed the challenge and was ready to take on something different from anything else I'd done.

'Since their last chief inspector, who clashed with management a while back, no one has really managed Search,' my superintendent said, 'so it will be good for your development.'

Perhaps I should have stopped to ask why no one had been managing the unit, but I was just pleased to have been given more responsibility.

The Search Unit weren't located within the Police Central Command in Lambeth like the rest of us, they were based a mile away near Tower Bridge. It was such a specialist area that many of us within the Met didn't know much about how they worked operationally, and that was the first thing I needed to find out once I took over responsibility for them.

The first thing I discovered, though, was that the majority of the unit was made up of inspectors, although not entirely. It seemed insane to me that while there was a shortage of inspectors on borough, there were more than a dozen of them concentrated in the search team. The other thing I couldn't help but notice was that the search team was once again entirely white and almost exclusively male, despite the fact that when they had operational needs they had officers of different ethnicities that they called upon from borough. Almost all of them had been on the search team for many years, and so they were self-managing, self-mobilizing, and in effect left to their own devices.

To get to understand their roles and their practices better, I decided to base myself out of their office two or three days a week, but from the very first day my interest in their work was met with a deep suspicion. I wasn't entirely sure why. I knew they had been used to managing themselves and they clearly viewed anyone new coming in with distrust.

'Cup of tea, boss?' one of them might say, appearing at my office door.

'Yes, thanks,' I'd reply.

'Er . . . any idea how long you're staying today?' they would ask.

'Probably all day,' I'd say.

Next time I went out into the office I would notice everyone had gone.

They clearly didn't like having me hanging around. Or perhaps they were just busy – in all honesty I gave them the benefit of the doubt. I knew nothing about how they worked, but that's exactly what I wanted to find out.

'Er, which days are you planning to be in the office this

week, boss?' one of the inspectors might ask on a Monday morning.

I'd tell him the days and then notice that on the days I'd given him I'd turn up to an empty office and sit there working alone all day, while they cleared off and did their own thing. So I was left with no choice but to surprise them and turn up on days when I'd told them I would be working in Lambeth. I quickly learnt this was going to be a game of cat and mouse. I tried to be open and give the impression that I hadn't picked up on their game – I had been an undercover officer after all and those skills did come in handy when managing a team – but I knew they were trying to pull the wool over my eyes. And as I suspected, on the days I turned up to surprise them they were all in the office, feet up on the desks, sipping cups of tea.

What I came to realize about this search team was that while their work was indeed specialized, when there weren't any incidents requiring their skills they didn't actually have anything to do. It seemed crazy to me that all these resources, all these great inspectors, were being left twiddling their thumbs by Tower Bridge.

I knew that if I wanted to make any changes I would need to get the team on board and take them along with me. I had spent enough time observing them to know that there were people within the Met who had spent years, perhaps decades, managing themselves, away from prying eyes, and my experiences on the Change Programme and in other areas meant that I always looked at a unit and wondered how I could streamline it to make it more efficient. Many of the changes I'd made to other commands had released a couple of inspectors back to borough, but I knew that these people would not necessarily be happy about that.

I had regular meetings with them, catching up on the jobs they had done and what they were working on each week. I had to tread carefully because they were already unhappy about me being there, so I was trying to get to know them on a one-to-one basis too, slowly trying to win each individual's confidence and clarify their thoughts on how the unit was working, and how they thought it might work better. However, most of them were close to retirement so they didn't have many ideas, and I knew I'd have a fight on my hands to make them accept any changes I might implement.

Eventually there was nothing for it but to call a team meeting, to discuss things as a group and gauge their views. We sat inside a small room, me with fifteen of them, including two women, all sitting round in a horseshoe shape. I explained why I had called the meeting.

'I want to present my vision to you of how I feel the unit can work more effectively and more efficiently.'

Silence. All eyes on me.

'This is a consultation period,' I continued. 'I want us to work together, so you can share your ideas and see how we can make that happen.'

Silence. A few people crossed their arms and sank down into their seats.

'I would also like you to move over to Police Central Command in Lambeth Road so that the entire Protective Security Command is based in the same headquarters and you can feel a part of the command.'

Fifteen stony faces stared back at me.

'What about all our kit?' one of them said. 'We're not moving over.'

'Well, we can find you space at—'

I didn't get to finish my sentence. Once one of them had spoken I suddenly felt the fury of the whole room. They were up out of their seats, standing over me, pointing in my face, talking over each other while I sat in my seat.

'Do you think you can come in here and try to change this unit?' one said. 'All the other chief inspectors just left us to it.'

I could see why.

'It's just because you're a chief inspector,' someone else said, standing up. 'You're just newly promoted and wanting to impress.'

'We know you've been on the Change Programme,' another said, coming towards me.

'Who do you think you are?'

'You don't understand what we do, you've got no clue!'

In the face of so much aggression, I tried to stay calm. I wanted to let them get their anger out. They felt threatened by me and I understood that and didn't take it personally.

'All I want you to do is have a look at my vision,' I said. 'None of it is set in stone. Think about how we can make it better, more efficient—'

Uproar again. They refused to discuss any changes, insisting I didn't know what I was talking about and that everything worked perfectly well as it was. But of course they thought that. They were a hidden unit with no management, able to come and go as they pleased. They were all highly skilled and, as a result, considered themselves untouchable. That department was one of the best-kept secrets in the Met, and now I understood why no one had gone in there, and why my superintendent had so readily handed me the job. They were antiquated, many of them close to retirement, and they were sexist, misogynist – there was no way they would be acting like this had I been a man. That unit was the epitome of what I had experienced throughout my career in the Met – white male domination. But if I wanted to drag them into the twenty-first century, it would have to be kicking and screaming.

Because above all, they were just angry. I felt that anger, and despite all the other times I had been in danger in my various roles throughout my career, for the first time in that room I felt intimidated. I tried not to show any emotion, but it was like being surrounded by an angry mob. The calmer I was, the angrier they got. I had to do something before my calmness was interpreted as weakness.

I stood up. 'Do not speak to me like that,' I said, in the most authoritative voice I could muster. 'That's enough. If you carry on like this you're going to get yourselves in trouble. I think we need a break.'

I told them that we would resume the meeting the next day, and that I wanted them all there.

The next day I went through my plan because I was nothing if not tenacious. They sat there opposite me, arms folded, faces set. I told them that I wanted to streamline the unit, making it into smaller teams, and that I wanted them to move into the central offices, not to be invisible any more, to be part of the bigger team, and feel a part of the Protective Security Command. I wanted them to get to know the other units and vice versa. In the interim, I wanted them to come to the senior leadership team meetings and update us on their work and the challenges they were facing.

But that was exactly the opposite of what they wanted.

No one said a word, they gave me nothing back. Thankfully I'd expected that so I set them a task and asked them to come up with some models and ideas and present them back to me in a week.

I went back to Police Central Command and told my superintendent what their response had been. It was he who had tasked me with this and said he would support me, so I hoped to get some advice. But now it seemed he'd changed his mind.

'You're upsetting Search,' he said, offering me no help whatsoever.

'I'm not upsetting them,' I responded. 'I'm dragging them into the twenty-first century as you wanted. Do you know what they do? No one has a handle on them. They are managing themselves.'

A few days later my superintendent told me that they had complained about me to the head of the Protective Security Command and insisted that they wanted me removed as their chief inspector.

'What do you want to do?' The commander asked me.

Did he think I was going to back down and do as they'd asked?

'I could complain about their behaviour,' I told him. 'They were extremely aggressive towards me. But I'm not going anywhere or complaining about them. They want the distraction and the drama and I'm not giving it to them.'

It was my tenacity to see projects through, to deal with difficult staff, that the Met had always admired about me, so the idea that they would suggest I back down now was ridiculous.

'I'll make my changes,' I told him defiantly.

So instead of stepping away, I actually spent more time basing myself at their offices rather than on Lambeth Road. The relationship wasn't an easy one. I did get them to come to the meetings twice a week, though they managed to block a permanent move to Lambeth Road when the commander suddenly decided the space I'd allocated for them was no longer available.

It was a really difficult time. The job was stressful, made more so by the units I was managing, and things at home were getting harder to manage as well. My mum had never stopped living with me throughout all my career changes, which had effectively rendered me her main carer. Over the previous few years, as I was working my way up in the force, Mum had suffered a series of mini strokes, each one taking another part of her away from us. It had been really hard to witness. As a result, and because of my long hours, I'd had to get people in to care for her, but even managing that was difficult. In the mornings I would wake Mum up as I got ready for work and then wait until they arrived around half seven before I left. I felt safe once I knew they were there to take care of Mum as we never left her alone. But balancing my duties as a chief inspector and my caring role at home took its toll.

And then, one morning in 2015, disaster struck. As I

was chatting to Mum she suffered a catastrophic stroke, right in front of me. Her arm just flopped, her face dropped, and she was completely unresponsive as if she were trapped inside her own body. In hindsight I was so lucky to have witnessed it, because it meant I was able to ring an ambulance immediately, though an image like that never leaves you. I held her in my arms until the ambulance arrived. As everybody knows, when someone suffers a stroke, time is of the essence.

I followed Mum to hospital that day, praying that she would be OK. My sisters and I rallied round, crowding around her hospital bed, hugging her, talking to her. Over the next days and weeks, work had to take second place as I and my siblings nursed Mum back to health. There were many things she had to learn over again – how to walk, how to talk – but I was my mother's daughter for a reason. We both had the same tenacious blood running through our veins. Mum eventually came home from hospital, a little more fragile than she had been before. She was paralysed on the right side, but at least she was home.

I of course had to tell my superintendent about what had happened and why I needed to take time off. He needed to know that I was Mum's carer – she was effectively my dependant. But my job was a busy one and there were lots of professional demands on my time, so it was often hard balancing the two sides, made worse by my aggressive and seemingly unfeeling team. At home I learnt how to use the hoist to get Mum in and out of bed and even ended up training new carers who came to the house so they could care for Mum in my absence exactly as I would. Eventually I found carers I was comfortable with and didn't feel the need to supervise. They became a part of the family and treated Mum as if she were their very own.

Then, on 14 June 2017, a very different disaster struck. A fire broke out in a twenty-four-storey block of flats in North Kensington. Grenfell Tower was an incident that shattered not just London but the entire country. Seventy-two people lost their lives, seventy-four people were injured (twenty seriously), and dozens more lost their homes and their possessions. The cause of the blaze which ripped through the building turned out to be an electrical fault in a refrigerator. It was a devastating moment in our capital's history, but in some way it marked a truce between me and my search team. I had always known their work was specialist, but the work that they had to do at Grenfell took its toll on them both physically and mentally.

PolSA was called in to search the building in the weeks after the fire, once it had cooled down and it was safe to enter. The amount of heavy equipment they needed to wear was tough enough, but it was my team's job to search every flat, every room, every corner for any bit of evidence that might help identify people. I could not imagine the strength of mind they needed to go into that building knowing what had happened there and how many people had perished in such horrific circumstances.

I visited the team at Grenfell on more than one occasion. I needed to make sure that they had everything they needed, both from an equipment point of view and from an occupational health perspective. Many of them required counselling after the scenes they witnessed, and I could see why. Even the first glimpse of Grenfell Tower on exiting the nearest tube station knocked the wind out of me. The building was still smoking for many weeks after the fire. As I approached, there were forensics tents lined up, and other tents for members of emergency crews to take a breather in. The atmosphere was chilling, the air still and quiet. Whether you were in the building working or not, just the vastness of it towering over you was enough. Outside on the ground, walls were covered in photographs of the missing or the dead, and those who'd lost loved ones continued to come to pay their respects.

'We'll show you around, boss,' one of the inspectors said.

I had to sign a register to be allowed inside the building, as well as wearing protective gear. We went up the stairwells, the same cramped, crowded, black and smoke-logged ones that those people had desperately tried to escape down. It was unbearable to try to imagine that night but your mind could not help it. The thought of these people made me weep. I couldn't stop my tears.

We went inside one of the flats, its walls blackened, furniture melted and misshapen, just the corner of a family photograph identifying its occupants amid the charred remains.

I left that tower with a renewed understanding, in awe of my search team that they could go into such a place day after day, week after week, and do their work. Because I had gone and taken an interest in what they were doing, we began to develop a mutual respect.

Grenfell Tower wasn't the only occasion I observed the Search Unit out in the field. Another time they took me to the site of a cold-case disappearance that they were investigating. It was in Epping Forest, a missing person who had seemingly disappeared without a trace. They showed me how they worked out the parameters of their search, how they explored every single item that lay on that forest floor in the hope of a breakthrough in solving the case. It was truly specialist work.

By that time I had been admiring for a while the voluntary search teams organized by Kent Police, and I had visited their units to find out more about how they were operating. Kent Police had their own staff search officers, but they also brought in volunteers, members of the public who had trained as police search advisers through Kent Search and Rescue. This seemed a great way to bolster our own resources. I worked with the organization to recruit some of their advisers to a newly formed Met Police voluntary search team. Working with them also gave us access to their equipment, which was in many cases far superior to our own and a huge bonus.

I decided that each volunteer search team would be designated to one of four geographical areas of London: north, south, east and west. If an incident occurred in their area, those volunteers would be mobilized for support. Just like the full-time search officers, these volunteers would be highly trained, so their support would be invaluable and would hand our own search teams five or six capable helpers on the ground to aid them. I took my plan to my commander who gave it the official rubber stamp and then I implemented it.

While my focus had been on getting the Search Unit more resources and understanding their work, the Threat Assessment Unit had been managed by my female inspector. We worked well together, but I knew my superintendent wasn't keen on her. It was strange for me to witness how he turned against her. It had started with something seemingly small. She had challenged him on a point of policy – a point I agreed with her on – and he hadn't taken it very well. I had come across many men within the organization who, once you crossed them, found it very difficult to move on. He just couldn't let it go.

'I want her out of my unit,' he said to me one day.

'No,' I replied, 'she hasn't done anything wrong.'

But I knew that she hadn't needed to. She had got under his skin, and that was enough.

She was an ex-protection officer and an ex-Police Federation rep. She was extremely well presented, extremely knowledgeable and assertive in a way that men enjoy mistaking for aggressive. I could see which way this was going to go. My superintendent was going to put pressure on me to find fault with her work, and in the absence of that he was going to bully her out. This was something I had witnessed often, mostly being a victim of it myself, and I was certainly not going to stand by and allow it to happen to someone else. Especially not someone who I considered to be good at her job.

I went to see the commander, though I wasn't surprised to hear from him that he had already received a complaint from the female inspector herself about the superintendent. Not that he had done anything about it.

'Oh, you know, he's having a hard time at the moment,' he said.

I became aware that my superintendent would be required to give evidence at a public inquiry. Many of the senior leadership team, including the commander, were concerned at the pressure he was under and wanted to protect him.

This, however, had nothing to do with his mistreatment of staff, and I said as much to the commander. Just because things were difficult at the moment didn't mean they could give him a green light to do as he liked. Turning a blind eye enabled and endorsed his bad behaviour.

I had always got on with my superintendent so I didn't feel comfortable about complaining about him, but I had no choice but to speak out. We shared an office at that time and we would often talk things through and support each other. He did have a bit of a temper and if he started raving at someone down the phone I would often mime deep breaths to him to help him calm down, which was always met with a smile. But even though I got on with him, I still always got the feeling from him that he didn't particularly like women in the force, and certainly not women who rose through the ranks. What I didn't know, though, was that other people had noticed that too.

In Protective Security Command we often wore plain clothes rather than uniform, and one day after a meeting, Cheryl Richards, a young black police staff member, started chatting to me. She asked me what rank I was.

'I'm a chief inspector,' I told her.

She looked surprised to hear this, and my own quizzical look back must have encouraged her to explain why.

'But why then does the super always consult with the other guy – what rank is he?' she asked. 'I've noticed it's a boys' club here.'

I was taken aback to hear her say this. I'd never said

anything of the sort around her so she must've picked this up independently. By 'the other guy' she was referring to one of the white men, an old friend of the superintendent's, and one of the boys' club members. I told her that he was an inspector, a rank below mine.

'So if you're more senior than him, why does the super always walk right past you and go straight to him? You seem invisible to him.'

I wasn't sure what to say to her, but sadly I knew that if she decided to continue her career in the Met then she would probably get to see for herself. It was something I had become used to, but I was still embarrassed that even the staff were noticing that my boss was ignoring me in favour of someone who was of a lesser rank.

Still, it was promotion season and I wanted to apply to be made superintendent, so that would make my rank equal to his. The only problem was that I needed my superintendent's support to be able to apply. One afternoon, as we were chatting in our office, I mentioned to him that I was interested in going for promotion.

He stared at me for a minute, across the desk where we sat facing each other. He didn't say anything at first, but then his face turned to thunder.

'Why do you think you're so special?' he asked.

I didn't answer him immediately, staying silent for what felt like a minute.

'Sorry,' I said. 'I don't understand what you mean.'

It wasn't that I thought I was special, it was that I knew I worked hard, and that I deserved a chance to progress in my career, and I had the evidence to prove I was ready. But even my intention to be promoted – to become the same rank as him – had infuriated him. It was such an abrupt change in someone I thought had become my friend. I couldn't believe this was happening to me again.

'Listen to me, Nusrit,' he said through gritted teeth. 'I had to wait years as a chief inspector before I went for my promotion. I failed four times at the assessment centre.'

But there was no minimum time any more that a police officer must serve in a particular rank before applying for promotion, you just had to have the evidence that you had performed at the next rank.

'It took me six years to get to superintendent,' he continued, 'and you think you can just go for it now?'

'But it's not about you,' I said.

I noticed after that day a turnaround in our working environment. I became invisible to him. There were no chats, no laughs, just silence in the office that we shared. He seemed to want to make my life as uncomfortable as possible – and for what? Daring to think that I, a woman of colour, could be the same rank as him?

A couple of weeks later I was away on a training course and my superintendent called me and told me I needed to send him some crime figures.

'But I'm away on a course,' I said, 'can't someone else do it?'

He insisted it had to be me. The ridiculous thing was that because I didn't have access to my office computer due to IT issues, I had to ring the office to get the figures.

'It doesn't make any sense,' the colleague I called for the figures said. 'Why don't I just give them to him?'

'He says it's got to be me,' I told him.

We were still sharing the same tiny office at that point, and when I got back a week later he came in and stood with his six-foot frame filling the doorway. He was so angry, red-faced, shaking a set of papers at me that were apparently so urgent a week ago.

'You're not fit for promotion!' he shouted at me. 'These figures are all wrong! I'm going to discipline you for this.'

I wasn't even sure what I had got wrong, he never said, but it didn't even matter in that moment, I was just so humiliated. The entire office had turned and was staring in our direction. When he stormed out, I got up and shut the door then hid inside for ages, too ashamed to come out when everyone, the whole unit, had heard him speak to me, their superior, like that.

I called my commander from my office with shaking hands. I was close to tears as I explained to him what had happened and what he'd said to me. 'He's got to stop,' I said. I was so angry.

'Oh, you know what he's like, Nusrit,' he said, 'he'll be all right. He's probably just in a bad mood.'

But why couldn't he see that this was targeted bullying by a superior? It was so obvious to everyone else. It was only the people who could actually do something about it who refused to acknowledge it.

I moved my things out of our shared office that day.

At around the same time my department was recruiting for a new member of the police staff, and the superintendent wanted to parachute one of his friends into the role. As they would be working for me, it made sense that I should oversee the recruitment, but the superintendent was insisting that an acting chief inspector should handle the recruitment himself. It made no sense to me, but I observed how they assessed the applicants. Some of them were really strong candidates. Three women in particular stood out to me: one who had been in a senior administration position within the NHS, another one who had a master's degree, and the third was an outside candidate, a highly qualified woman of colour from the private sector. Cheryl wanted to apply, and the acting chief inspector told her he would let her know when it was advertised, but then didn't; she only found out from me when the ad had gone out. These were all highly qualified people, but they had two things going against them: firstly, they were all women, and secondly, they were all women of colour.

I was there with the superintendent and the acting chief inspector when the latter was going through the applications.

'This one can't have it,' he said, 'she can't even make the interview because she's got to pick her kids up from school.'

He screwed up her application.

'And this one,' he said, raising another application, 'she can't even write on a piece of paper.'

This was rubbish. 'Let me see that,' I said, reaching over. I knew all of these women were highly qualified, I'd seen their applications myself.

'There's only one person for the job,' he said, clearly referring to the superintendent's friend.

'You can't make up your mind without everyone being interviewed,' I said.

The superintendent just sat there smiling and agreeing with him.

I could hardly believe what I was witnessing. This was everything that I had complained about through my career in action, old-school officers rejecting new blood, women, people of colour, in favour of their old friends. It was nepotism at its most repellent.

'I'm taking over the recruitment process,' I told the ACI after the meeting. 'You're not even responsible for this unit. I'm the one who has to work with this person you're recruiting.'

'No you're not,' he said, shaking his head and gathering up the applications.

'But I should be doing this,' I insisted.

But he flatly refused my involvement. He then complained to the superintendent, who wrote an email to me insisting that the ACI would be recruiting even though I would be taking over the unit.

This was a complete conspiracy, all just to shoehorn their friend in. I was outraged. I went to the commander, even to HR anonymously, and told them what was happening, insisting to them that these women were being discriminated against. It undermined the integrity of the whole process. I told them the comments that had been made about these women, comments that I considered sexist and racist.

But the person I spoke to in HR refused to act.

'No, it's fair when we bring people in from outside the unit to make judgements about them,' she said.

'But it's not just about the comments he's making,' I said, 'it's about the integrity of the recruitment process in general. How can you make up your mind about someone before you've even interviewed them?'

I even took it as far up as Lucy D'Orsi, who was the deputy assistant commissioner, but it felt as if the Met were closing ranks, as usual. They talk the talk but don't walk the walk.

HR insisted it was perfectly acceptable to ask people you knew to apply for roles, so it came as no surprise to me that the white man, with whom they were all friends, got the job. Even though I had been a whistleblower, my anonymity had not been protected, so now I was seen as a troublemaker and the superintendent wanted me out of his department. I put in a grievance against him which was undermined by the bizarre terms of the investigation which breached standard operating procedure. During this time the superintendent was promoted to a different command where I later learnt that he continued the same pattern of behaviour towards another senior colleague, Syed Hussain, with whom I had worked previously. He too put in a grievance against him.

It was at this point I started speaking to Lawrence Davies, an employment lawyer I had met through the Black Police Association, and he told me I had a strong case, so I started to compile an employment tribunal against the Met simply because the official process was not working for me.

Meanwhile, more generally, my time in Protective Security Command was becoming more and more difficult, and not just in terms of my relationship with my superintendent, who by now knew about my complaint to HR. Caring for Mum was a full-time job that I did around the hours of the job I had to do to pay the bills. I was often left feeling that I was neglecting Mum and her needs for the sake of the job that I was married to. Each morning felt like a relay as I waited for the carers to arrive to take over from me, and then of course I waved them off when I arrived home from work in the evening after a long day.

Not only that but the terror threat London was facing at that time was deadly serious, so we could afford to leave no stone unturned in terms of our threat assessment work.

On 3 June 2017, just ten weeks after the stabbing of PC Palmer, the capital suffered yet another devastating incident. A van was deliberately driven into pedestrians on London Bridge, and it crashed on Borough High Street, just a few hundred yards away, where three men leapt out of the van and started stabbing members of the public. Eight people were killed and forty-eight were injured including four of our own officers who had tried to stop the attackers. ISIS later claimed responsibility for the attack. London was shocked, London was grieving, we all were, and yet we had a job to do to ensure this could never happen again. At a time of such threat to our national security it was, of course, all hands on deck. We were all on duty, all leave was cancelled. We worked twelve-hour shifts to manage the situation. Sifting through the intelligence we were receiving had suddenly become more vital than ever.

The work was exhausting, particularly as it concerned the command in which I worked more than any other. Between us we were working 24/7, and one morning my superintendent called a meeting at 7 a.m., before his shift ended and an hour before ours started, to do a handover. The timing of the meeting made life really difficult for me, and my superintendent knew it. Mum's carers didn't arrive until 7.15 a.m. But my boss was insistent that we were in the office for seven. In the end I didn't know what to do, and in my panic I left home early that morning leaving both Mum alone and my house unlocked so that the carers would be able to gain entry. I ran to the tube station, even tripping over in my haste, and arrived at the office for the meeting sweaty, dishevelled but — thankfully — just in the nick of time.

'I made it,' I said, panting. 'Shall we start the meeting?'

'Huh?' the superintendent said.

'Where's the acting chief inspector?' I asked.

My superintendent looked at me. I saw that familiar fury mounting behind his eyes.

'I'm not responsible for his trains!' he barked at me.

What else could I say? He handed over to me and left. My colleague eventually rolled in just before eight.

'Where have you been?' I said.

'What do you mean?' he replied. 'The boss said to come in whenever I could.'

I realized then that he had deliberately got me in early knowing how difficult that would make life for me.

Another time he actually did the complete opposite. I was at home one morning when I got a call from one of the office assistants in the command.

'Where are you, boss?' she whispered quietly but urgently down the phone. 'Everyone is here for a meeting, the commander, even the DAC. You're the only one who isn't here.'

I knew my superintendent had done this to me on purpose. This was undermining my role, and it was bullying. These occurrences were never admitted to, but the Met would later say that either way it was a very minor matter. Of course all the senior leaders would notice I wasn't there, but I wasn't going to let him beat me. Instead I got ready quickly and dashed into work, somehow arriving just in time for the meeting to get going. His face was a picture when he saw me there.

'What are you doing here?' he asked.

'Well, I've come because everyone else is here,' I said, gesturing to all the people who had taken their seats ready for the meeting.

I wasn't going to be put off my promotion. I decided to go ahead with the application but instead of going back to my superintendent I went straight to the commander. I told him what was happening to me under the superintendent and how he was blocking me for promotion.

'I don't want him anywhere near my application,' I told the commander.

He nodded. I thought he would respect my request, but instead he told my superintendent, and took my entire application with him.

A few days later, the commander asked to see me.

'I spoke to the superintendent about your application,' he said. 'You're going to need to change that example because he says that he doesn't remember you doing it.'

I couldn't believe I was here again. It felt like Groundhog Day.

'Really?' I said. 'He doesn't remember it?'

The commander shook his head. 'Sorry,' he replied.

'But when I wanted to go for that role in Royalty and Specialist Protection, he endorsed that very same example so that I could transfer. That was only four or five months ago,' I said, 'so what's different now? How does that work?'

He was quiet for a moment, then said, 'I'll ask him.'

'I *demand* an answer,' I said, feeling the combined fury of all the other times a white man had tried to block me getting to assessment.

'I'll find out,' the commander insisted.

But he didn't find out. When I asked again a few days later, he told me that the superintendent hadn't replied to him. He had effectively refused to answer the commander's question, then. But in reality I didn't need to know what was happening – hadn't I seen this happen enough times before to recognize it by now?

In the end the commander supported my application for promotion himself, so later in 2017 I returned to the assessment centre to do my scenarios once more. The board that marks scenarios is made up of senior colleagues and community assessors (community members who are trained assessors) and they are paired up to observe each scenario and they mark you accordingly. There is an opportunity, before you go in for the assessment, to see a list of the names of those who will be observing you. If you have had any previous history or a conflict of interest with any of those names, or you feel that they might not be neutral in assessing your work, then it is possible to state that you do not want them to mark you. That way, everybody can be sure that you were assessed fairly.

I waited in a tiny room before one of my scenarios and was handed the list by an admin assistant.

'Is there anyone here that you feel has a conflict of interest?' I was asked.

I recognized a couple of the names on the list from SO15 – Counter Terrorism Command – who I had worked with when the senior managers there were making my life difficult.

'Yes, I don't want either of these two people to assess me,' I said, marking their names on the list.

I sat waiting for the actor who was coming in to role-play with me and was getting myself ready when the two assessors walked in and sat at the back of the room. I stared for a moment. There was a black woman, the community assessor, and a white man who I immediately recognized as one of the names I had just pointed out on the list, one of the people I had said I absolutely did not want assessing me.

For a moment I looked around, unsure what to do. The two assessors were settled in their seats, waiting to go, clipboards in hand, and then the actor arrived and introduced himself. It was about to start. I still wasn't sure what to do. It didn't make any sense. Why would they have allowed him in when just moments before I had said he was one of two people I did not want marking me? But there was no time to think, everyone was gathered, I would just have to accept it. And so we started.

I did three scenarios – thankfully for the other two I had different assessors – and an interview that day. All in all I felt I had performed pretty well. Despite the initial setback I was confident that he couldn't have found fault in my performance.

When I received my marks a few months later, I found that I had failed the promotion. This had never happened to me before at the assessment centre, I had always scored top marks. I went through the paperwork trying to figure out what had gone so wrong, and it seemed that I had failed on my psychometric profiling test. This was a test that many people believed was unfair to minorities and women, so I had already decided to appeal before I even looked at my results from the assessment centre, but when I did I could not believe it. I had scored top marks in every single scenario I had done, fives across the board, apart from the one that had been assessed by the man I had not wanted there, where I received a three. It was potentially that low score that had contributed to my fail. I was devastated.

I posted my appeal immediately, alerting the appeal board that I had been assessed by someone I felt had a conflict of interest. My appeal was upheld, but I was still curious to know more about what had happened with the lower score in the scenarios. As it happened, a few weeks later I saw the community assessor from that scenario, Angela, in the corridor at the Empress State Building. She stopped me as we passed each other.

'How did you get on with your promotion?' she asked me.

'I failed,' I replied.

'What do you mean? You did really well.'

I told her about the psychometric tests, and how I was appealing. She nodded, knowing as a black woman herself that the tests didn't have a great reputation.

'And how did you get on in the scenarios?' she asked.

'I got top marks in every one,' I said, 'apart from the one you marked.'

'Oh, I had a real battle on my hands that day,' she said.

'How do you mean?'

'I've been assessing for twenty-three years,' she explained, 'but I've never had that happen before.'

The sadness and confusion on my face must have encouraged her to explain more.

'Every time I said you'd done really well, he would say, "No, she didn't."'

'Really?'

'He doesn't like you, does he?'

She was right, he didn't, and he'd just made it public. My instincts had been correct. We would later say he was never told that I'd objected to his being my assessor. He also said he believed his scores to be very fair.

Six months later my appeal was successful. I had to go back to the assessment centre and repeat the scenario with two new assessors. I scored top marks in all the scenarios. Finally, I was made a superintendent. And yet again I'd only got my promotion after I'd raised a grievance because someone had tried to stop me in the first place.

A Regulation 13 notice is served when an officer is thought to be 'unsuitable for policing'. In her review, Baroness Casey noted that Regulation 13 notices are 'disproportionally served on Black, Asian and ethnic minority probationers' and these same people were disproportionately resigning. In fact, an interim report on the Met's internal misconduct system revealed that between 2018 and 2022, when compared with white officers, black officers were 126 per cent more likely to be subjected to a Regulation 13 notice, Asian officers were 123 per cent more likely, and mixed ethnicity officers were 50 per cent more likely. Yet while BAME officers were more likely to be found 'unsuitable for policing' they were also more likely to raise a grievance than their white colleagues; in fact, for black people it was four times more likely. Why is this important? We don't know the ethnicity of the person they raised the grievance against, but given what I experienced with the white boys' club I would take a wild guess that the grievances of BAME officers are more likely than not to be against a white colleague.

In her review, Baroness Casey wrote how they had found

> a culture of discrimination that takes many forms in the Met but is felt most acutely by those who cannot hide their differences from the White male norm, particularly people of colour and women. We have found racism, misogyny and homophobia in plain sight. The 'resistance to difference' emerges in a culture of bullying experienced by a significant minority of the organisation . . . Those who do not conform to the prevailing culture face discrimination, bullying and barriers to thriving and progressing in their careers. Those who try to conform teeter on a knife edge in the organisation. If they speak out, they will be labelled as a 'trouble maker'. They are incentivised to hide things about themselves which would bring them into conflict with the prevailing culture. But even if they walk that line effectively, the organisation may still decide that their 'face doesn't fit'.

So what *is* the prevailing culture? It is exactly what I found. The culture is white and the culture is male.

'There is a profound culture across the Met that incentivises people to look, act and sound the same, and a resistance to difference,' stated the review. 'The "boys' club" culture, particularly in the specialist commands, creates a vicious cycle,' Baroness Casey observed. 'The more male-dominated the command, the less women seem to be able to break through.'

Somebody once said to me that the Met resembles a pint of Guinness – all white on top. That always seemed like a good analogy to me.

Some white people within the force would deny it, but these micro-aggressions, these incidents of having promotions blocked, of being unfairly assessed, or failing to get a posting, are all too common to black and Asian staff within the Met Police. When I was superintendent, there were only nine of us BAME officers who were working at the very top of the organization, either in superintendent roles or as chief superintendents, but there was something else which was even more concerning. At that time, half of us were either under investigation or had been under investigation. It felt like a hostile atmosphere to be working in as an officer of colour. Almost all of us had experienced the kind of everyday racism I had become worryingly used to during my time in the Met; but being in fear of investigation, seeing how white officers were protected and black and brown officers were much more likely to have misconduct charges levelled at them, created a climate of fear among us. People might think 'if you've done nothing wrong, there is nothing to fear', but we could see for ourselves that was not how it was working. Instead we wondered who among us would be next. The odds were concerning, and it felt like the higher black and brown officers got in the force, the more chance they had of being picked off. I felt sure that if Commissioner Cressida Dick could see what we were concerned about and how things were stacked against us, she would step in.

I decided that we should form a crisis group of BAME senior officers to bring this to the attention of the only people who could help us – those at the very top of the Metropolitan Police. At that point in time there were no black or Asian assistant commissioners, and just one Asian deputy assistant commissioner, Neil Basu, so we were the highest-ranking officers of colour.

Crisis groups – or Gold Groups, as they are known – are common within the organization and usually happen when there is a critical incident or a tribunal. One person will chair the group – which in this case was me – and the aim was to tell the commissioner how we were feeling. We wanted her to hear what we had to say, and take action, because we felt that if such discrimination could happen to us at our level, it would also be happening to people at lower ranks.

I organized a meeting, attended by most of the senior BAME officers at that time, either in person or on Zoom. Each of us introduced ourselves in turn. I invited the commissioner to join us, but she didn't come, and neither did any of her senior colleagues. Instead she sent her representative who, whenever we directed our experiences to him, just put his hands up and said, 'I'm only here to listen, I'm not allowed to say anything.'

It felt frustrating. Here we were, as many of us as possible gathered in a room to talk about the racism we had experienced within an organization that promises to protect and serve all citizens. But how could it do that if it couldn't even show up for its staff?

'There is institutional racism at the heart of the Met,'

I said. 'If this is happening to us, what's happening to those in lower ranks?'

'I can't respond,' Cressida Dick's representative said, 'but I will take away the minutes of the meeting and discuss it with the commissioner.'

Nothing came of it. Nothing was acknowledged. In my mind Commissioner Dick should have been horrified that her most senior BAME officers were gathering because they wanted to highlight the racism in her force. But she didn't even write to us about it.

When Baroness Casey's review was published in March 2023 and the new commissioner Sir Mark Rowley stood outside New Scotland Yard, he insisted he had not been aware of any racism within the Met. Perhaps, though, the force was just guilty of not listening to those of us who were trying to speak out.

9

Wood Green

It was spring 2018 when I emerged from the underground and walked up a slight hill to Wood Green Police Station for my new posting. The station itself is located on the High Road in Wood Green, a four-storey Victorian redbrick building with cast stone around its bay windows.

As I approached my new workplace that morning, my mind was sent spinning back a decade to the last time I had been on borough, as we call it – meaning back in a local station. Then I had been a newly qualified sergeant, eager to earn the respect of my officers. Now I was returning to borough as a superintendent – but other than that I wasn't sure how much had changed.

The car park was filled with patrol cars, a few uniformed officers stood around smoking cigarettes, and I could already feel a buzz about being back on borough. I went in through the main doors, past the custody office as detectives were bringing in prisoners and the custody sergeant was reading them their rights, and on up to the second floor where my office was based.

Returning to borough after spending so long in specialist policing had felt daunting. I hadn't applied for the job, rather I had been posted to where I was needed most operationally. When I was posted to Haringey, I felt a little anxious, but mostly excited. It had been a decade since I had been involved in operational policing; I had spent the last ten years sitting in meetings that were protected by the Official Secrets Act. I had been in the vanguard against some of the biggest threats this country faced, and sat with some of the most dangerous criminal gangs doing business. So what was it about being forward-facing again that felt so terrifying?

The Haringey Command was made up of three boroughs – Haringey, Edmonton and Enfield. There was one chief superintendent who oversaw the entire command, and four or five of us superintendents who were each responsible for our own units. The response team dealt with emergency 999 calls, and had four teams, A, B, C and D, just as it had been on my first ever posting at Leman Street. Another superintendent was responsible for CID, another for Neighbourhood, and another for Safeguarding. My role was HQ, and the task assigned to me due to my experience with the Change Programme was to deliver a new North Area Command that would amalgamate all three boroughs. The Met were in the process of creating four new commands that would cover the capital in its entirety: North, South, East and West. The reason for this was that it would create more officers at the disposal of each command: rather than them working solely in their area they could be dispatched throughout the entire command. It also meant more streamlining at the top end of management, as it wasn't necessary to have that many chief inspectors, inspectors and sergeants in each borough.

Wood Green Police Station came as a pleasant surprise to me. There was a nice, friendly atmosphere there, and I felt it instantly. It was a relief not to have to brace myself for a rough period of settling in. I realized that being back in borough might actually give my career a new lease of life.

I was met by one of the superintendents as the chief superintendent was away and he was acting in her role. He told me that until very recently they had been a small team of three superintendents.

'We're a very close-knit team,' he said, 'we all gel very well, though we don't want to come across as cliquey. We've just worked together for a long time.'

'I understand,' I replied.

I took this as encouraging. He was welcoming me into the team, letting me know how friendly it was, how strong their bond was. I could understand why that would be when they had been working closely together for so long, all of them senior managers. My arrival, along with that of Fard (who was responsible for Response) a few weeks earlier, meant that not only had their team swelled from three, but it had also swollen to include two people of colour which, considering the demographic in that part of London, made perfect sense.

After a few weeks, Fard and I were presented at a local Independent Advisory Group (IAG) meeting run by different members of the Haringey community. These IAGs were there to hold the police accountable, and the chief superintendent very proudly introduced the members to their two new brown superintendents – up until then, after all, they hadn't exactly been representative of the community.

One of the women on the group said, 'Where are your black members of senior leadership?'

'Well, Nusrit and Fard are there,' the chief super said.

'No, where are your black leaders?' she repeated.

Everybody felt a bit uncomfortable. The chief superintendent didn't know what to say and stuttered. But I could see she had a point and I gave her a knowing smile as I agreed with her. It made sense that the community wanted to see a force which reflected their different ethnicities.

I wasn't given any induction or support while settling in at Haringey. I didn't even have an office, but I didn't mind that. In specialist units like SO15 all the offices were open plan and I knew that sitting with your staff was the way you built relationships.

The task I had ahead of me in terms of amalgamating the boroughs was huge though. There were 2,000 members of staff (both officers and police admin staff) who would need to be accommodated into the new structure. I started a consultation period, going around and speaking to each member of the team, having drop-in sessions and being available and visible, and letting them know what my vision was and how we would achieve it. I also consulted a friend of mine, Paul Martin, one of two black chief superintendents who had successfully introduced the West Area Command. I had first come across him when I was in the Protective Security Command; he was invaluable when I was having problems with my superintendent. We had become good friends after that, so I reached out to him to guide me through the process of creating the North Area Command. He had one inspector who had been particularly integral to the process and he released him to come and help me go through it.

Many of the staff were apprehensive about the changes, as I'd often found was the case when implementing large-scale reorganization. I knew I needed to take them with me on this idea so during the consultation I invited them to come and meet with me and offer their suggestions or preferences. But it wasn't just the staff that I had to consult with, it was the public too. They needed to be reassured that any changes to their local police unit wouldn't mean an inferior service. And before presenting my plan to the community, I needed to present it to the chief superintendent.

After I had delivered the reorganization, the deputy assistant commissioner came and congratulated me on a job well done.

'It was a seamless transition, Nusrit,' he said, 'well done, you've delivered the most successful programme, the smoothest in the Met.'

The measure of its success was the fact that out of the four newly created commands, the North Area Command received the fewest complaints and appeals from staff. I had managed to keep most of them — and I knew it was never going to be all of them — happy.

In my days as a sergeant in Islington I had felt it was important to be seen on calls and to be out on the frontline alongside the officers. I still understood that it was the only way to build respect among the rest of the command, so in Haringey, whenever my time allowed, I would go out on calls with the area car or in the police van, or sometimes Fard and I would even go on foot patrol. We knew that as two uniformed officers we would be stopped (the public had no idea of our rank, they just saw two officers), and we often had to deal with petty crimes like shoplifting or reporting a stolen car, but it was a good way of not only building trust across the whole of the command but getting to know the community better.

I knew that whenever I went out in the van or the area car, the officers would feel nervous. I was conscious that they would feel that I was watching them, though I was also aware that it worked the other way round. They were watching me too.

One day I was in the area car in Tottenham, north London, when we received a call that a teenage boy had been robbed at knifepoint. He was only seventeen, and had been selling clothes online. He'd arranged to meet some people who were interested in buying his trainers one evening. This was a very risky thing to do as this area at night is not a particularly safe place. The CAD room had given us directions for where to meet him, only as we drove up and down we couldn't locate him.

'Let me get out and walk,' I said. 'I'll find him better on foot.'

'No, boss,' they said, 'you're not walking round here. Stay in the car.'

I laughed to myself, thinking of the nights I'd spent walking alone in Whitechapel as a new recruit. No one had been concerned about my safety then – if only they knew.

We located the teenager beside a parade of shops, and while my officers spoke to him, I went into the surrounding shops to ask if any of the shopkeepers had witnessed anything, or whether they had CCTV cameras that might have caught the robbery. I surprised myself how much I enjoyed being back in frontline policing again, and the best thing for me was that I didn't have to do the huge amount of paperwork when we got back.

Slowly but surely, the teams understood that I wasn't afraid to get stuck in, and that earned me their respect. In fact, sometimes they had to hold me back. On another occasion we were called to attend an address where a fight had been reported. We located the house and I was already out of the car.

'Come on,' I said, 'let's get in there.'

But again they held me back.

'Boss, hold on, let's wait for other units to arrive, and we'll go at the front, not you.'

For this reason, not only did the teams respect me, they also liked me. I was also quickly gathering a reputation as someone who was approachable, who could help them sort out issues or advise on promotions.

Another thing I was given responsibility for was professional standards. That meant if a complaint was made against an officer, or there was any situation involving North Area Command staff, it would be my job to investigate it. Sometimes a member of the public might complain about how they were handled by an officer, or perhaps they felt the reasons they were given for stop and search were dubious. It was my job to call in the officers and question them. Often an officer would justify their own behaviour towards a member of the public by saying that they were being difficult, or that they'd aggravated the situation by insulting or attacking them.

But I noticed that when I asked for their body-worn camera footage, they would make some excuse. They had forgotten to turn it on, or they'd only remembered to turn it on halfway through the incident, so there was no way of me seeing what the context was or whether their response was justified. 'The body-worn cameras are there to protect you as much as members of the public,' I warned so many officers coming into my office. I reminded them of the policy, that the camera must be turned on for every interaction with a member of the public. 'As soon as you get out of your car you should be turning your camera on. If you come here again and say the same thing then I will need to give you words of advice.' 'Words of advice' is a low-level sanction, in effect a disciplinary, and it can stay on an officer's record.

In terms of my frontline policing, I couldn't have been happier. There seemed less office politics out in borough, less ego than in specialism. Your rank automatically earned you respect. You were the boss, and your word was final. My whole career had been a struggle, not because of the policing work but because of the white male ego, which thankfully didn't feel a part of this type of policing. Not since I was a rookie at least. It felt like finally I could concentrate solely on providing a good service to the general public.

As ever, though, the weather didn't stay calm for long. Within the bowels of Wood Green Police Station, in an area reserved for staff, hung a noticeboard showcasing the management structure of the borough. At the top of the 'tree' was a photograph of the chief superintendent, and underneath was a row of photographs of the five of us superintendents – three white men, myself and Fard, who was on the end.

One day, a few months after I'd arrived in the borough, I walked by and noticed that Fard's portrait had been defaced. Staff or officers – obviously we didn't know who – had drawn phallic symbols on his photograph. Not on any of the rest of us, only on Fard. And they hadn't stopped there: the same graffiti was visible throughout the station, on the walls, in the stairwells, in the lifts. It was pathetic, like being at school. How could grown men or women be doing this? I was staggered. But what worried me more than anything was the fact that it was Fard, one of only two superintendents of colour at the station, who was being targeted. It had to be a racist attack from within our ranks, which meant we had a racist officer within our command. That was something, as head of professional standards, that I needed to address immediately. Fard was a victim of a hate crime and should be treated as such.

I took photographs for evidence. I didn't want Fard to hear about it on the grapevine as he was off on annual leave and not due in until the next day. When I told him, he was upset and shocked, quite naturally.

'And was it only my photograph that was defaced?' he asked.

'Yes,' I said.

He, like me, agreed that it must be an incidence of racism.

He thanked me for telling him, but I think both of us were left feeling unsettled in some way. Why wouldn't we be? We had clear proof that there was racism within our command. And what message had it sent to our staff? Dozens of BAME members of staff would have passed by that photograph and seen the graffiti. How had that made them feel about working from this station? How did they know whether or not it was their own colleague who was responsible for this? And had it been their colleague, how would they feel going into dangerous situations alongside them, knowing they needed their fellow officers to have their back? It was also imperative to consider the effects this might have on the public. If there was a racist officer among us, how safe were they? We had no idea, so this had to be investigated.

I went to see the chief superintendent, who had, by now, returned to her role.

'This is unacceptable,' I said. 'We need to have a strong response to this and let the entire command know that it is out of order and will not be tolerated and that those responsible will be held accountable.'

But she was unconcerned. Her first response was: 'Who told Fard?'

'I did,' I said.

'You shouldn't have done,' she replied.

'Sorry, boss?' I was surprised and angered by her response.

'You don't know that it is an act of racism,' she said, 'you should have just arranged for it to be removed. It would have been better for him not to know to save his feelings.'

'But if he is a victim of racism then he needs to know, and he needs to be treated as a victim,' I insisted. 'Not telling him just disempowers him.'

I was glad I'd told him. The boss came across as cold,

detached. I wondered if she was even hearing what I was saying because we were clearly coming at this from completely different angles – me as a woman of colour who had experienced racism her whole life, and her a white woman who just wanted to sweep it under the carpet and instead reprimand me for telling the victim.

'Just get someone from the professional standards team to go around the station every morning and every evening and wipe it off,' she said.

'But what does that tell our other members of staff about how seriously we take racism in our command?' I asked.

It worried me that having a racist within her ranks was of no concern to the boss. She didn't want to take positive steps to find out who it was, to tackle it head on and let the entire command know that racism of any kind would not be tolerated. The only thing I could think was that she was completely in denial about institutional racism in her force, and the reality was, of course, that as a white woman it simply didn't affect her.

Just recently I'd had another issue with her. I'd heard from a black inspector that he was being bullied by his white chief inspector. He had confided in me what had happened – it was the same old, same old: micromanaging his time, refusing to allow him to do flexible working hours so he could gain his masters degree. The crux of it was that he was being denied requests that any other officer would've had approved easily. I had spoken to his superior and warned her that if his complaints continued I would need to take further action. I'd told her that I would monitor her. But instead of taking my warning on board, she had gone above me to the chief superintendent and complained about my conversation with her. I had been pulled into her office and asked why I had spoken to her and when I explained about the allegations of bullying the chief superintendent refused to let me deal with it.

'He doesn't fit into the Met anyway,' she said.

'What do you mean by that?' I asked. 'I don't like your insinuation or your tone.'

Though I was never sure what she meant, I think she was alluding to when he had left previously to run a business abroad before returning to the force. It frustrated me that I couldn't help him. It felt so wrong. But I was also scared. I knew how things had often panned out with my other senior BAME colleagues, and if I tried to pursue this bullying claim, I could be accused of bullying the white chief inspector myself. Once again I was being asked to just wipe away the racism.

It seemed to me just another example of white privilege. She had never had to deal with racism whereas I could bet that, like me, Fard had been dealing with it his whole life. We *knew* what it looked like. But what could I do except what she had instructed?

I had a feeling that this problem wasn't going to go away. In fact, something quite sinister was festering within our station, though I didn't know that then.

Late in 2018, one of the other superintendents announced that he was leaving. That left his unit – Neighbourhood – in need of a new superintendent and I thought it might be a good sideways move for me to gain more experience. Neighbourhood had always looked interesting. It's a very front-facing job, and you need to be able to deal with the community. The role required holding surgeries so they could come to you with their concerns, liaising with the council and heading up things like the Independent Advisory Group, or the Stop and Search Scrutiny Group. It was a tough job, but I thought it would be a good chance for me to return to the public-facing work I loved, so I went to see my chief superintendent to let her know that I was interested.

'I'm not sure, Nusrit,' she said. 'You've only just got here.'

'I'm not sure what you mean by that, boss,' I said. 'I've been here nearly a year.'

She had said the same to me a few weeks before when I had asked to be put forward for the new round of promotions. She'd also said the same to Fard, telling us both we weren't ready. The white female chief inspector who had been accused of bullying by the black inspector and who had been at the station less time than me was being supported in her application for promotion. I maintained my calm on the outside but I was absolutely fuming to find that I was yet again not valued, yet again rejected. I was starting to doubt myself.

'No,' she said, 'I'm not going to give you that job. I don't know how the public would react to you with a mic in your hand.'

'What do you mean?' I laughed. 'What assumptions are you making about the communities in Haringey?' To this day I wonder what she was insinuating. Perhaps she thought I'd lead the community in some kind of riot? She later said she meant that I had not put myself into scenarios where I could readily demonstrate my ability to engage with the local community. She would also deny telling me that I wouldn't be given the job if I applied. Either way, at the time I got the sense that she felt very negatively about the people we were supposed to be serving. She had already told me that she didn't like the Labour MP for Tottenham David Lammy, that he was obstructive and aggressive. These seemed to me like racist stereotypes about the people in the community we were meant to be serving. She would later deny that these comments were made or inferred.

'And anyway,' she continued, refusing to explain herself, 'I've already got someone in mind.'

She told me that she had approached this female superintendent specifically about the Neighbourhood job. It was someone she already knew. Of course it was. But I wasn't going to let her get away with it.

'But you haven't advertised it,' I said. 'There needs to be due process.'

But her mind was made up.

It was a couple of weeks later that I mentioned it to Fard as we went out for a walk one day.

'I spoke to her about that job too,' he said.

'Oh my God, really?' I said. 'Unbelievable.'

I was laughing and crying at the same time. How on earth did the chief superintendent think that we didn't talk to each other?

I was surprised Fard wanted it. This was already his second superintendent job, and his previous one had been Neighbourhood. There's no way the chief superintendent could say that he didn't have the experience.

'What did she say?' I asked.

'She said "It's not for you".'

'She's got someone lined up for the position,' I said.

I told him what she'd told me. Fard was furious.

'But where is the due process?' he said. 'That woman isn't even already here, we are; she hasn't got operational experience, we have. I've even got experience in that role.'

'I know.'

It was depressing to realize that, even at this level, nothing had changed. It seemed that if you had the right colour skin, you got fast-tracked through the ranks. You were nodded into jobs and handed promotions. None of those things happened to BAME officers, and the incidents I knew about, or that I'd witnessed first hand, were starting to stack up.

But after almost thirty years it was starting to wear me down. Usually when I was knocked down I would get up and fight harder, but now I felt tired, battle weary.

Fard went to see the chief superintendent. He told her that we would put in a grievance if she put that woman into the role without allowing us to apply, without due process. After all, she had already refused to support both of our promotions. He also went to the Superintendents' Association, told them how unfair it was, and they agreed to put pressure on our boss to make the process fairer. It was probably thanks to their support that the chief superintendent was forced to allow us to apply, but how many more times would we have to fight for our right to apply for a job? How many more times could we bear it? She then decided, as she was soon going to give way to a new chief superintendent in the North Area Command, that it should be the incoming person who decided who should have the job. That seemed to us like a fairer process, and at least we had secured the right to apply. Other than that we would just need to wait to find out who would get the nod.

One morning in February 2019 I arrived at Edmonton Police Station just before eight o'clock. As I walked through the secure areas, something made me stop. Then, as I realized what it was I was looking at, I went completely numb. What I was standing in front of was a swastika. It had been daubed on the wall overnight. It was about eight to ten inches tall and about five feet from floor level, right in my eyeline. I stared at it, then looked around, as if searching for someone who could confirm that what I was seeing was real. Could there really be a swastika graffitied inside the secure areas of a police station?

In that moment my worst fears were realized. I was absolutely convinced that graffiti was there because we had failed to take action about the defacing of Fard's photograph – we had, by our inaction, told the vandal that it was acceptable. It also confirmed to me that my instincts had been right. How could a swastika not indicate that we had a racist officer among our ranks? Now my chief superintendent would have to take action. I went straight to her and told her what I had seen.

'We need to keep this between us,' she said, getting up and closing the door.

'What do you mean?' I said, barely concealing the anger on my face. Was she for real? 'I'm head of professional standards, how can I not act on this?' She had tied my hands before, but not this time.

My boss just sighed.

'I don't want you to talk about it,' she said. 'This stops here.'

'But why?' I asked. 'We have four superintendents, of course they need to know if there is a Nazi floating around the station.'

'You're being over-dramatic, Nusrit,' she said.

'Over-dramatic? Someone has painted a swastika in the police station. What are we going to do about it? This has gone too far now.'

'We're not going to talk about this and you're not to mention it to anyone.'

But I told her I didn't feel safe, that I felt the community wasn't safe. 'And what about our black and Asian officers?' I said. 'How do they know that the person they're patrolling with is not the person who drew that symbol?'

She refused to take the matter any further.

It felt as if she was sweeping it under the carpet, just like she had before, but why? Did she, just like the Met on a wider scale, not want to admit that there was racism within her ranks? She insisted that once again it would be cleaned off and that we wouldn't be telling anyone. This was wilful blindness.

'It needs reporting,' I insisted.

But even though professional standards was my remit she told me that I would not be liaising with Central DPS (the Directorate of Professional Standards). This would be done by her. Once again she was obstructing me in the carrying out of my job. Over the following months I often asked for an update on the investigation but none was forthcoming. It was starting to look like a cover-up. She later stated that she had been told that she should not inform others about the then ongoing investigation in order to minimize the chances of compromise.

It wasn't until March 2020, more than a year later, and long after that chief superintendent had left, that Ben Hannam, a probationary officer working out of North Area Command, was arrested for terrorist offences. A database leak from an activist organization investigating Iron March, a neo-Nazi terror outfit, found his name among a list of users and subscribers to the group.

Hannam became the first British police officer to be convicted of terror offences, including lying on his application and vetting forms upon joining the Met, and being in possession of two terror documents detailing knife combat and how to make explosive devices. Chillingly, he also pleaded guilty to possessing an indecent image of a child. He was jailed for four years and four months. He'd arrived at the station two months before Fard and me.

Central DPS never linked the swastika to Hannam (as far as I know, it was never linked to anybody), though in November 2019, when news of the swastika appeared in the public forum, the incoming chief superintendent – who claimed she had never been briefed about it on her arrival – said at a Haringey community meeting that it may have been made by builders working at the station. As far as I knew at that time there were no such builders. The Independent Office for Police Conduct (IOPC) also confirmed they had not been informed of the incident and expressed surprise at that. The Met insisted that a DCI had been assigned to investigate it but as 'no forensic opportunities were identified' they were not able to establish who had drawn the graffiti.

I felt a sense of irony, then, when in 2023 the Met commissioners announced their commitment to targeted action in their turnaround plan, 'A New Met for London'. They stated: 'We commit to targeted action and reforming our Professionalism Command to make sure we root out individuals who discriminate and reduce disproportionality in how we handle misconduct.' When I think about how fervently I was told to keep quiet about the graffiti, I find it hard to see how discriminatory individuals will be brought to light.

Baroness Casey's review recognized that there was a culture against people speaking out within the Met. One case study, referred to only as H, spoke from her perspective as a black woman:

> Throughout her career in the Met, H says she has felt unable to complain due to her race and gender, and a fear that she would be labelled as a troublemaker and either ostracised or moved.
> 'You have to try and be invisible as a Black woman . . . If you complain you get a reputation as being trouble and then supervisors try and pass you on to other teams.'

This was certainly what I experienced during my time.

Another anonymous case study within Baroness Casey's review was a woman, 'L', who had been sexually assaulted numerous times by a male colleague. She said that he had 'forcibly started to undress her while they were on duty together, and only stopped when a member of the public drove past. On another occasion the officer masturbated in front of her in the communal changing room.' Only, when she reported him she was dissuaded from pursuing a criminal case against her attacker and told that it would be reported in the media and then 'everybody will know'. Instead she reported it as a misconduct, providing a video interview and a full written statement to support her claim. It was only 'by chance', months later, that she found out from a colleague that the case against him had been dismissed. 'L spoke to DPS (Directorate of Professional Standards) and challenged their decision but was told "it's your word against his", and that her abuser had a "long, unblemished career in the Met". No further action was taken against him. He has since retired from the Met.' The woman told the review: 'Everything I went through, the worst thing I did was report him. If I could go back now I wouldn't report him.'

But I believe the culture of secrecy within the Met, of punishing those who spoke out, extended more widely than gender and race. One gay officer who had been the subject of lewd comments by his colleagues felt that his promotion and transfer opportunities had been blocked as a result of him speaking out against wrongdoing. As one interviewee put it in the Casey review, 'Women and men who did speak out found themselves being informally punished for it, with micromanagement, being given undesirable tasks, being excluded or bullied in the workplace or moved to another team without asking. Complaining meant: "you're likely to be ostracised, restricted, likely to go sick, moved to another borough".'

The Met has a long history of punishing whistleblowers. Back in 2014, the *Guardian* newspaper reported that senior officers had made three separate attempts by letter to stop PC James Patrick speaking out about the manipulation of crime statistics within the force. In one letter they insisted he should be barred from having any contact with members of the public and he was told he would face disciplinary action if he continued to speak out. PC Patrick claimed to the BBC that the Met 'puts reputation before the truth', though as a result of the evidence he submitted to the Public Administration Select Committee, the head of HM Inspectorate of Constabulary and the then commissioner, Sir Bernard Hogan-Howe, were forced to admit that the manipulation of crime figures was taking place.

'The most depressing part of our inquiry is the way in which the Metropolitan Police have treated my constituent, PC James Patrick, who was our key witness,' said Bernard Jenkin, the chair of the committee. He also called for an overhaul of protections offered to whistleblowers.

Fast forward eight years, and following the IOPC's report into the disgusting behaviour of officers at Charing Cross Police Station, Susan Hall, the chair of the London Assembly's Police and Crime Committee, said that whistleblowers within the Met should be granted anonymity in order to tackle the 'culture of silence' within the force.

It was early spring in 2019 and the chief superintendent's time was coming to an end. I hoped that the incoming boss would want to take matters like the graffiti in hand. It seemed to me that there had been a litany of incidents that needed addressing. On the chief superintendent's last day I had my final meeting with her. She asked me how my time under her tenure had been.

I paused, aware that she might just want me to be polite, brush everything under the carpet, but I felt that this was the last chance I had to impress on her what I had found disappointing. She needed to know the areas I felt that she had misjudged. After all, she was going on to a promotion, and I didn't want her to make the same mistakes in her next role.

'I'm sorry,' I said, 'but the way you treated that black inspector who was being bullied was appalling.' I then began to list occasions where I felt she had been negligent and, in some cases, downright ignorant.

She stood for a moment with her mouth open and it became clear that she hadn't really been asking me to tell her what I thought of her leadership. And how dare I do that to her!

'You stood in the way of me doing my job and refused to let me act on some serious crimes committed within our stations,' I concluded. 'There is institutional racism here and you haven't done anything to address it.'

I knew perhaps I was speaking out of turn, but she needed to know how she was treating people.

'Are . . . are you saying I'm a racist?' she said, seemingly appalled at the suggestion. Her eyes filled with tears.

'It's not my job to give you a certificate or a badge to say you're not a racist.'

'Oh,' she said, dabbing at her eyes.

I sat there, dumbfounded. I didn't know what to say. I couldn't exactly get up and comfort her, though I had a feeling that was what she wanted me to do. Maybe she wanted me to make her feel better. But I couldn't. She'd asked me a question and I'd told her the truth. So I just sat there for a few minutes and then left.

Back in my own office I got straight on the phone to Fard.

'Oh my God, I just made the boss cry,' I said. 'She asked me whether she'd been a good leader.'

'Don't worry,' Fard said. 'She asked me the same question the other day and I told her what I thought too.'

I knew what we were both thinking. She had weaponized her emotions against us. White women's tears are well known to black and brown people. They are a tactic used to muster sympathy and avoid accountability, often trying to paint people of colour as the aggressor. I couldn't believe that I had just witnessed that from my chief superintendent.

That was the last time I saw her in the office. She went out that afternoon for a long lunch to do her handover with the new chief superintendent. I hoped that her departure would mean a new start for me. Part of me wished I could be a fly on the wall at that lunch. I could only imagine what she would be saying to the incoming chief about me, but I was ready to deal with whatever came my way.

The new boss was also female – and white, of course. I had crossed paths with her over the years, and when I'd heard she'd got her promotion to chief superintendent I had emailed to congratulate her, though I don't think I realized at that time that she would be coming to North Area Command.

Her arrival marked a new beginning at North Area Command, and one of the first things she needed to do in her new role was to appoint a new superintendent to the Neighbourhood role

There were three of us who applied for the role: me, Fard and the female officer our old boss had originally lined up for it. The incoming chief super asked us each to apply in writing, so I committed to email a persuasive case for why I felt the job should be mine. I wrote in it that one of the reasons I was so keen to take over responsibility for Neighbourhood was because I was seeking promotion and I felt that it would help me to have experience in another area within the command.

When the new boss interviewed me for the role I reiterated all of this. I felt that I had done well in my interview, all I could do now was wait and see who she chose.

Within months of her appointment to the role, the boss brought over a newly promoted superintendent with whom she had worked at her previous command. He was nice, a decent guy who would be heading up CID, only he didn't have an office.

'You can share with me,' I said.

'Oh thanks, Nusrit, are you sure?'

'Yes, no problem,' I said. 'It'll be a bit of a squeeze but we can make it work.'

I knew what it felt like to be the new person without an office, so I didn't mind at all. An office was still a luxury to me.

It wasn't long after that that the chief superintendent called me one night to let me know that I hadn't been successful in getting the Neighbourhood job.

'I'm going to give it to the best candidate,' she told me. 'I've looked at your CV and the two of you haven't got that experience of Neighbourhood.'

I was disappointed, but it was obvious she was going to give the job to Fard, and I could see her logic. At least we had secured a fair process, even if we'd had to fight for it. He had previous experience and was the right person for the role.

Fard took the job and moved into the office next to the boss, which had always been traditionally where the Neighbourhood superintendent was based. But we didn't have much time to luxuriate in this new, fair appointment. It turned out that the candidate our old boss had originally picked for the Neighbourhood job was coming over to Wood Green anyway. She would now take over Fard's old area, Response. I had not even been asked whether this was an area I wanted to move into.

'I'm going to look after her,' the new boss said. 'I want to give her all the support I can as she's coming from specialism.'

I thought back to my arrival at Wood Green after leaving specialism myself. That hadn't been my experience at all. Nobody supported me or gave me extra care or help; I was left to my devices and I had to suck it up. The blatant difference in the way we were treated played on my mind.

'I need to have her near me,' she said, explaining that she would take Fard's new office.

'But that's the Neighbourhood office,' he said. 'It always has been.'

'I know,' she said, 'but I want to give her all the support I can.'

But Fard shook his head, refusing to give up the Neighbourhood office. I was pleased to support him in standing his ground, but in the end it didn't matter. When the new superintendent arrived, Fard came in and found her sitting behind his desk.

'The boss wants me next to her,' she insisted.

He agreed to share his office, as I was doing with the other new superintendent, but it turned out that wasn't going to be good enough either. Each morning Fard came in and found this new superintendent sitting behind the desk with his name on it. She would arrive early and move all of his things to another, smaller desk.

'What am I going to do?' he asked when we went for a walk.

'You'll just have to come in earlier than her,' I laughed.

'But that seems really pathetic.'

'She's trying to force you out of your own office,' I said. 'Don't let her. Fight, Fard! For the sake of your desk!'

We both burst into laughter. The situation was farcical: two superintendents fighting over a desk, and a third one helping with the repossession of it. But at least we could joke about it.

He did as I suggested, but after a few weeks it started to feel too childish to him as she started coming in even earlier.

'I can't do it,' he said.

He gave it up, and the chief superintendent got her way.

I know how hard it is to hold your own when the institution works against you. I have written a lot in these pages about the 'old boys' club', but there is a more insidious club within the Met, and it is that of the white female clique. Privileged-background, public-school-educated women who protect their own, promote their own and tell themselves that they are promoting diversity as a result. These women do not mentor BAME women or working-class women, they do not take us under their wing, and they do not insist that our offices should be beside theirs. I've seen just how they can mobilize if one of them is facing any kind of roadblock in their career, or wants to get promoted, but I've yet to witness that power being unleashed for a BAME candidate. I called those women the 'Mean Girls of the Met' because at the time it felt just like the 2004 Lindsay Lohan movie. At events you see them huddled together, surveilling the room, never a woman of colour among them. Look at the very top of the Met's ranks – it is almost completely white. This is not because BAME people have not tried to make it, but because they have been filtered out.

In May 2019, the Met celebrated the centenary of women officers being allowed into the force. Hundreds of female officers gathered in St James's Park to march. Three out of the five most senior-ranking BAME officers at that time attended: myself, Parm Sandhu and Shabnam Chaudhri. Also in attendance were Cressida Dick, who was then commissioner, Helen Bull, the assistant commissioner, and Lucy D'Orsi, the deputy assistant commissioner. What a statement the Met would have made if its most senior white women had marched alongside us, but instead we watched how they huddled together. Even on a day celebrating women in the force, the divide was clear. For them, it would always be us and them. Moments later we were told we would be marching at the back, behind them – but we did at least manage to photobomb their selfie.

Our new chief superintendent had only been in the role a couple of months when she needed to go away for three weeks for a course. On the day she was due to leave, she sent an email to let us know that the newly promoted male superintendent she had brought over from her last borough would be stepping up in her absence.

'Have you seen her email?' I said to Fard.

Though we were both outraged by what we were reading, by this point nothing surprised me. This man was newly promoted into his role and yet he'd somehow leapfrogged the rest of us more experienced superintendents to be promoted to acting chief super. It made no sense whatsoever.

Fard and I went to her office and complained immediately, both of us asking why she had not advertised the opportunity.

'You knew that I was interested in promotion,' I said, 'an acting position would have really helped me.'

'Oh, I didn't realize you were interested in promotion, Nusrit?' she said.

'You did,' I insisted. 'I wrote to you about it when I applied for the Neighbourhood role.'

I even went back to my office and sent her the email to prove it. At this point in my career I knew how important it was to have everything in writing for the inevitable moment when I'd have to prove what I'd said. To this day she maintains that I had never suggested I should've been given the opportunity.

'Oh well, I've given the role to him now, but I promise that the next time I'll give you two the opportunity.'

This wasn't good enough. I had been facing this exact same problem my entire career, and now that there was a new chief superintendent I had convinced myself that things would be different. But here we were again, and I found myself nearing breaking point.

Fard was determined to take it further, and threatened to put in a grievance. The boss agreed, begrudgingly, to allow Fard to step up into the acting role for one week while she was away.

'What about me?' I asked her.

'I don't think you're ready for promotion yet, Nusrit,' she said.

'On what basis? Have you even looked at my evidence, my examples?'

She looked a bit uncomfortable. 'No,' she admitted. 'You're right, I haven't looked at your examples.'

So on what basis had she decided I wasn't ready? I realized then and there just how much her long lunch with the old boss had cost me.

I was now finding it ever harder to pick myself up for the fight, but I decided to speak to the Superintendents' Association. They had helped Fard and me in the past and hopefully they could again. I was assigned an officer to speak to, and I told her that I didn't want to stay in North Area Command any longer. I wanted a move out. I could already see I had no career prospects there.

'You need to speak to your chief superintendent about this,' she said. 'You should stay at North Area Command and mediate with her.'

'I can't,' I said, confused as to why she couldn't see that

it had already gone beyond that. 'The odds are already stacked against me there.'

'But your chief superintendent was a mentee of mine,' she said, explaining that she was like a daughter to her.

I couldn't believe what I was hearing. There was clearly an outrageous conflict of interest here. It was not possible for her to aid me in my grievance if she regarded the person I was complaining about as close as family.

Fard had also put in to leave the borough. He had been my only friend there and I wondered how I would cope without him. I think both of us were just exhausted, demoralized, tired of the endless struggle we had both been engaged in throughout our careers. While the institutionalized racism within the Met wasn't always explicit, not necessarily direct or something you could quote, it was relentless, day after day, week after week, month after month, year after year – and now, for me, it was becoming decade after decade. I was just so battle weary.

My new chief superintendent's comments had made it clear to me that I was going nowhere under her watch. My career was effectively over unless I could get a move out of the borough. She would later say that she neither denied me the chance of promotion nor denied career support. I told my boss that on welfare grounds I would be requesting a posting out of North Area Command.

I was due to have an operation on my ankle around the time that Fard would be taking over as acting chief superintendent. I was off sick but I knew we were short-staffed and I wanted to support him, so I agreed to work from home while I recovered. On the boss's return, I was still healing from my operation, but the workload she set me to complete from my sick bed was totally unmanageable. I couldn't cope. It made me dread my return to work because I had seen how this had played out so many times before, how so many colleagues before me had just been overwhelmed with work until they couldn't cope any more. I didn't want to fall, or fail, but my mental health was suffering.

I went to speak to my GP and told him about everything I was having to cope with. I sobbed in his office and for the first time let all my emotions out. The years of abuse had finally caught up with me. This was not like me – I loved my job; I had always loved the job – but it was just becoming unbearable.

He diagnosed me with PTSD (post-traumatic stress disorder), which was a huge turning point for me. It made me feel heard, as if someone had acknowledged for the first time just what I had been dealing with, not just now but for a long time. He signed me off work with stress, and I went home. It felt like admitting defeat – I was a fighter not a quitter – but something had to change.

Nearing the end of my sick leave, which had lasted a month, I refused to go back as long as my chief superintendent was still there and so they had no choice but to post me elsewhere. I was actually posted to East Area Command. At the same time Shabnam Chaudhri was leaving East Area, and she invited me to her retirement do. I got special permission from the Superintendents' Association to attend. Otherwise I knew that if I went to a leaving do when I was sick, someone would report back and I could very easily face a disciplinary.

I'd received an email from the commander in the East Area a few days before, telling me that he was looking forward to me starting on the unit. And at the leaving do he came over and introduced himself. I had never met him face-to-face so I hadn't recognized him.

'I understand you're currently off sick,' he said, shaking my hand.

'That's right, guv,' I said.

'Yes, your chief superintendent has already spoken to me about you. I've also spoken to her predecessor. We had a good chat.'

I stared at him, unsure what to say in response, but the blood must have drained from my face, and certainly my legs were shaking. If he had spoken to both of my most recent chief superintendents I was under no illusions as to what they would have told him. Suddenly I found myself on the back foot before I had even started.

I just gave him a nervous smile and asked, 'And what did they say?' I then immediately regretted posing the question and found a reason to hurry away.

I made my excuses and left the party. I knew then that I would not be going to East Area Command, and sure enough, a few days later I was told the post was no longer available. The commander had insisted that he needed someone there now, that he had no idea when I would return from sick leave, and so the post that had been assigned to me had been taken by someone else.

10

New Scotland Yard

I had visited the renowned New Scotland Yard in the course of my three decades in the Met, but in December 2019, when I arrived to find my desk there, it was my first time being based at this iconic building. I had been told to report for duty to Deputy Assistant Commander Stuart Cundy who at that time was working on a project on professionalism. It sounded like an interesting area, particularly given my experience in professional standards at North Area Command. I knew very little about what I would be doing until that first day.

It had been a stressful few weeks. The *Sun* newspaper had published a story about the Met being hit by a series of racism claims by senior BAME officers. The newspaper had named me as one of the people who had started an employment tribunal against the Met, along with reporting that Chief Superintendent Parm Sandhu was suing for prejudice, and Chief Superintendent Jeff Booth was suing for wrongful arrest. Acting Chief Superintendent Novelett Robyn Williams, Chief Superintendent Paul Martin and Superintendent Ricky Kandola were all facing misconduct investigations. I was devastated that my name had been leaked to the newspapers, but even more devastated that it had been the rep from the Superintendents' Association who had leaked it. For me the employment tribunal was a private matter; I hadn't spoken about it even to my friends, and certainly not to my family. Now everyone knew. I was the subject of corridor conversation now, colleagues giving me knowing looks but not saying anything. I was still coming to terms with having to take that action against the Met and I certainly wasn't ready to read about it in red-top newspapers. It was a deliberate act, and a violation. When I complained, the chief super from the Superintendents' Association insisted that she'd never spoken to anyone at the *Sun*, though she had spoken to two other journalists 'off the record'. She then referred herself to the DPS, but the damage had already been done, my name was already out there. And so it was with this cloud hanging over me that I arrived at New Scotland Yard. I was past the point where I could get angry any more, I was just numb. Nothing was a shock or a surprise, and I prepared myself for the worst.

I was met there by DAC Cundy.

'I'm really sorry,' he said, shaking my hand. 'I've just been told that you've returned from sick leave. I had no idea until yesterday that you were coming here.'

'Oh,' I replied.

'Don't worry, I'll think of something for you to do.'

He showed me to a desk up on the second floor. I

looked around me. There were many people I recognized buzzing around the floor. I was relieved to at least see faces I knew, and sometimes I was able to put a name to them, or say hello. Only just a few desks from mine I saw someone else I most definitely knew: my first chief superintendent from North Area Command. This was the woman I had famously made cry on her last day, the woman I felt had blocked my promotion, who had told me to keep quiet about the swastika. She looked up and our eyes met for a brief moment. We didn't so much as smile at each other, and I quickly looked away. I currently had an active grievance with this woman – why on earth had they put me to work just yards away from her? I had arrived at New Scotland Yard excited to see what it held for me, but suddenly I felt intimidated, unsure. I tried to hold my head high, just as I had done many times before.

A few minutes later DAC Cundy appeared at my side. He'd had an idea about what I could work on and invited me into his office to discuss it. I was relieved to step away from my desk.

He wanted me to work on producing a paper on how to create better career pathways for black and Asian officers. I was pleasantly surprised. It was, of course, my passion, and I was encouraged that the Met were now willing to turn their attention to this issue. I had a chance here to make a real difference in this area.

'The only thing is,' I explained to him, 'I did this two years ago.'

'Did you?' he said.

I explained to him what had happened after my superintendent exam, and how I had written to head of HR

Clare Davies expressing how psychometric testing discriminated against BAME officers. I had made suggestions in the document about how best to help those same officers map out their career paths in the Met.

'Oh, OK,' Cundy said.

'I could rehash it?' I suggested. 'Maybe speak to some serving officers of different ranks, ask them what they feel would help them to progress in their careers?'

I didn't want to miss this opportunity to create real change for officers coming up through the ranks. DAC Cundy agreed, so I set to work.

I loved the work – I even loved working out of New Scotland Yard, the very epicentre of British policing – but it wasn't easy being in that office. The floor was full of officers who either knew all about my tribunal, or were actively involved in some way. One of these people was a commander who had been charged with responsibility for the crisis group that had been formed as a result of my employment tribunal. The Gold Group would meet to strategize, looking at the issues I had raised and considering how the Met could best move forward as a force. As the person they were all discussing, I was not invited to attend. Having this officer in such close quarters made life extremely awkward, particularly when she would stop talking and stare as I walked by. When I went to use the photocopier, or to make a cup of tea, I often saw her huddled together with my old chief superintendent and the chief superintendent I believed had leaked my name to the press – the very people I had made accusations about in my tribunal. Sometimes they were in the lift and would stop talking as I got in. Other times I just let the doors close on me and waited for the next one. I'd see them huddled together, whispering in corridors as I walked by. My *Mean Girls* analogy was becoming more and more real every day. Later, one of the chief supers explained that they were only whispering as it was an open-plan office and they didn't want anyone to overhear. She added that she never saw me while she was speaking to other commanders at New Scotland Yard. It was like some bizarre nightmare, and I couldn't help but wonder if it was a deliberate intimidation strategy. It took a lot of resilience in the face of that to keep turning up each day, to tell yourself these people couldn't possibly be talking about you and that you were just paranoid. I had spent my entire thirty-year career witnessing groups of white women just like these ones, as a new recruit at Hendon all the way up to superintendent at Scotland Yard.

I was relishing the work so I tried not to let those women get to me. I had been busy collecting testimonies from sergeants, inspectors and chief inspectors all the way up to superintendents, and to be honest what they all said to me gave me the courage to face those women because their experiences were so similar to mine. All the officers I spoke to said the same: that they had never received any mentoring, that their career paths had never been mapped out in the same way they saw with their white colleagues, and that they had suffered for speaking out about the racism they'd experienced. There was widespread recognition of the white clubs, the men and the women. They too had stories about how they had seen them look after their own and overlook BAME officers. They too had had to fight for their right to be promoted or to apply for a job that was never going to be advertised because a white person had been lined up for it. It had happened on an endless cycle, and our collective exhaustion was overwhelming.

I knew that institutional racism existed within the Met Police. I had experienced it myself, and I had seen other colleagues suffer as a result of it, but working on this paper also made me realize that nothing was changing even at entry level. Thirty years on from when I had arrived in the force during their drive to make it more diverse and representative of the community they served, new recruits were still coming up against the same prejudices and the force looked practically the same. I felt the weight of all these careers on my shoulders – every person who had been discriminated against, and isolated from an organization that was supposed to care about people. Could this paper and my recommendations help change that?

I decided to speak to DAC Cundy about how I felt in the office environment, and the behaviours I'd noticed, which were only getting more blatant on a daily basis.

'Oh, I'm sure that's not the case, Nusrit,' he said, dismissing my concerns with ease.

'But this is how I feel,' I said, 'and the Met has put me into this environment.'

He shook his head.

You see, this is what people do. They don't see these micro-aggressions, and tell us it's all in our heads. But after a lifetime of experiencing small acts of racism you would think we might know what we're talking about. Yet *still* those who have no experience of this tell us we must be imagining it.

If he was right, if I was paranoid, it was for good

reason. My fears were based on my experiences of putting my faith into an institution that was diverse in name only. It made me more determined than ever to make waves with this paper. It had the potential to finally show them, to finally cut through their denials.

Baroness Casey's review did not look too closely into how women or people of colour progress in their careers within the Met. She simply noted that their progression is disproportionate compared with their white counterparts. But if she had, I wonder if her recommendations would have tallied with mine. I wonder if she too would have decided that nothing will change until there is accountability at the very top.

I recommended that the head of every Operational Command Unit should be answerable to whether his or her BAME staff are progressing through the ranks. It should be in their best interests to make sure that they are receiving promotion, or getting postings. They should be held accountable and it should be a part of their performance indicators. The other officers I spoke to confirmed what I knew, that there were no career paths mapped out for them, that they weren't in receipt of mentorship. This was what needed to change. My experience of being supported by Shabnam all those years ago made all the difference in saving me from a stagnant career. This was an experience that white officers had constant access to. I wrote in my report that every BAME officer should get a development plan once they pass their two-year probationary period. Their chief superintendents should ensure that they get access to secondments, and that they move around the command to develop their professional experience and 'round them out' – a phrase we hear so often as an excuse for why we're not supported in our desire for promotion.

I also wrote that BAME officers should be given more opportunities to act up. In fact that should be a key part of their plan. I wanted to see commanders having to be answerable to panels, and one another, in terms of how many of these opportunities they have given these staff. The panels would assess how many BAME staff under their command went for promotion, what the commander did to assist them, how many acting-up opportunities they carved out for them, and how many secondment opportunities they had. That way, I wrote in my report, you would be able to see who was getting through, and who wasn't. For those who weren't successful, you would be able to see exactly what had been put in place for them, what extra help they had been given. If their BAME officers weren't moving up, then commanders would need to explain why that wasn't happening under their watch.

I handed my report in to Stuart Cundy. Perhaps some might think that a person of colour would have been better placed to head up diversity and inclusion rather than a white man, but for me the sex or colour of someone is nowhere near as important as the commitment and drive they need to have to do the job, and do it properly. I handed my paper to Stuart and hoped that he would read it and perhaps incorporate some of what I had said into policy.

And then I waited. And waited. Days went by, then weeks. I didn't really have a role now that my paper was finished and I found myself at a loose end. I supported Stuart, would help him with odd jobs, or find figures, but

I was a superintendent acting as a personal assistant to him. All eyes were on me as I tried not to put a foot wrong. I knew they were waiting to catch me out and pin something on me. I was extra diligent, my eyes wide open.

He never gave me any feedback on the paper I'd written, no one did. I don't know if it was even read. In the 2023 report 'A New Met for London', the commissioners stated their own hopes for reforming their promotion process. 'We'll make the way we assess performance and the way we promote people fairer and more transparent and provide incentives for our people to develop themselves. We will recognize people who change our culture for the better, changing our promotion and development policies so they align to our expectations and inclusive behaviours.'

My report, and all the battles I had with my superiors over the course of my career, tried to do exactly what the commissioners' report laid out. The only difference was that I was victimized for trying to highlight the very issues the Met are now striving to correct.

That period of time, sitting in that New Scotland Yard office with nothing to do in the company of the women I felt had conspired to land me there, aimless, ate away at me. I really did love my job and I wanted to get on with it, but I now found myself in no-man's land and I wasn't sure how much more I could take. I would wake up each morning and brace myself for the day ahead, wondering what micro-aggression I would have to face, watching my back to see what hostile act would be levelled at me. This had been the case for my whole career, but this time

I didn't have meaningful work to throw myself into. I was, at that time, the most senior Asian female officer in the Met Police (Parm Sandhu had already had a gross misconduct levelled at her and, although she was later cleared, she retired from the force in 2018; Shabnam had left too) and the reality was I did not feel safe at all, I did not feel protected. I felt vulnerable and exposed by the institution I had served loyally for thirty years, one that kept quiet about racism within the force, and one that had told me to keep quiet about it too.

I would go home and see Mum's smiling face. I would put my head in her lap and tell her all about the things that had happened. I knew she didn't understand and couldn't answer back. Throughout my career I never complained to Mum though I had often asked her advice about which jobs I should apply for or the promotion process. She would help me make sense of it all, she would tell me to fight for what was right. Now, though, since her strokes, all she could do was look at me and give me a smile. Perhaps the fact that I was finally telling her what was happening – what was *really* happening – meant my time really had come to an end.

In February 2020, I handed in my notice. I felt that I had been left with no other option. Lawrence Davies, the lawyer handling my employment tribunal, agreed that I had no choice: my working environment was untenable, and my prospects for promotion were zero. In my view, I was effectively constructively dismissed, and I was not required to work a notice period. The effect the toxic atmosphere was having on my mental health was skyrocketing, and I knew it was time to go. My happiness and wellbeing was too big a price to pay. I had given thirty years of exemplary service and if things had been different I would still be there doing the job I loved and devoted my life to. But I couldn't escape the fact that it was a job that had failed to protect me from abuse and had let me down countless times. It's like they always say, the job won't love you back.

My last few days working for the Metropolitan Police were emotional ones. I was required to go to Charing Cross Police Station to hand in all of my uniform so that it could be disposed of. As I did so, my mind couldn't help spinning back to all those years ago at Hendon, when I refused the skirts they tried to pass across the counter. What had happened to that feisty young woman who had insisted that she wear trousers and had triggered a uniform change for all female officers? Even the commissioner, Cressida Dick, wore trousers now. Did she realize she had me to thank for that?

Everybody who leaves the police having completed their thirty years is entitled to a Leaver's Certificate which commemorates your exemplary service to the Met. This is presented to those leaving the force by the commissioner at a special ceremony in New Scotland Yard. My instinct was not to attend the ceremony, to just leave quietly without my certificate, but as I reached the end I felt the need to celebrate a career I had loved. Surely I had earned that. It hadn't worked out as I had hoped, but I knew I had created positive change, and fought for what was right every step of the way. I made up my mind to attend, but an invitation was never extended. Instead my certificate came in the post to my home address. It was another punch in the gut.

I was also required to hand in my warrant card – a card

that I had kept at my side night and day since it was handed to me at Hendon – to Deputy Assistant Commissioner Alison Pearson. To mark my length of service, the DAC invited me to go and have a cup of tea with her in her office on my last afternoon. I appreciated this gesture so much because I felt at a loss for what had happened. I still couldn't believe I had been forced into this position and out of a job I loved so much. This would give me a chance to go gently, and give me a sense of closure. I knew from other officers that it is always an emotional moment handing over your warrant card and I was grateful that at least I'd be able to do that in the sanctuary of her office, away from prying eyes, or those women on the second floor.

But in one final gut punch, I received a call from her staff officer saying that DAC Pearson could not make it. He suggested instead that I meet him by the lift on the second floor. And so it was there, in a most unceremonious location, that my career with the Metropolitan Police came to an end. A man I had never met before came to take my warrant card and my eyes filled with tears. I felt them roll down my cheeks. This card had been with me for a lifetime – it was a part of me. We both stood there in silence. He didn't know what to say and I didn't really want him to say anything. He eventually took my warrant card and my police Oyster card and escorted me from New Scotland Yard, as is customary.

I stepped out on to the concourse in front of this iconic building. It was a beautiful scene. The River Thames stretched out ahead of me, and on the other side of it the London Eye glinted in the sun. I turned around to take one last look at the pale stone-face of the building, an iconic landmark of the capital. My eyes welled again with tears – how could they not? I had given my life to the force, I had been proud to be a police officer. I hadn't chosen this career, yet in some way it had chosen me. My identity was tied to it. Now it was time to de-institutionalize myself and allow myself to heal.

11

The Outside World

Life changed in 2020, not just for me but for everybody. A few weeks after I walked out of New Scotland Yard for the final time, the country was closed down due to the Covid pandemic. I hadn't planned on finding a new job straight away – I knew I needed time to decompress – but I perhaps didn't realize how much time I needed to process everything I'd been through.

Mum's health had continued to worsen over the last two years since her last major stroke. She was confined to bed, looked after by carers. I caught only glimpses now of the feisty woman she had been, in sounds she made objecting to something I'd given her to eat, or the way she was being washed, the odd word she said, or if she managed a smile or made her carers laugh with a gesture that was so defiantly her. But for the first time since I was a teenager I had time to be with her, time that my job had not afforded me. As I sat by her bedside talking to her or holding her hand, or helping to get her washed or changed, I grieved that this was all I had left of her, that she had faded away while I was working. Why had I waited until now to spend time with Mum when there was so little of her left? Each day it was painful to watch her, but at least she was still with me.

I might have left the Met but the institution still ran through me. I'd catch myself in conversation referring to the Met as 'we'. If I was in the street and a police car went by, I couldn't help but wonder what was happening or what it was responding to. If I'd seen an officer in trouble I would have gone to their aid without a second's hesitation. Being a police officer hadn't just been a job, it had been an identity, and now I needed to start all over again. The last time I'd felt like this I was twenty-one and fresh out of university. It was a strange time. I tried to concentrate on new skills and hobbies. I even taught myself how to ride a bike. That might seem strange, but I'd never had the opportunity to learn as a child as it wasn't my mum's priority, and this was a new challenge for me.

My employment tribunal was ongoing, but due to Covid my lawyer was told by the Met that they didn't have the manpower to investigate my claims and so any correspondence kept getting delayed and delayed. The best advice I received from fellow officers who had been through the system was to put it to the back of my mind, and so I did. I boxed it up and forgot about it. There was nothing I could do but wait.

It was a few months later that my thoughts started to turn to what I was going to do to make a living. While I was still inside the Met I had seen many officers who handed in their warrant cards on a Friday and started a new job in private security on the Monday. They had used their notice period to network, to line themselves up with high-paying jobs. There was an idea among the force that our skills were very much in demand in the outside world and that private companies would pay highly for them – though this wasn't my experience. Due to my abrupt departure, I hadn't thought to line anything up for myself.

I started to apply for security jobs for private companies, roles in diversity and inclusion, even counter terrorism work for the government. Initially people would be excited to hear from me, but then they would mysteriously go cold. I began to worry that they were Googling my name and seeing the *Sun* article where my name had been leaked. Was that what was putting them off?

My thoughts turned to teaching. I was aware that a lot of ex-police officers now trained new recruits and I had often mulled over my own training – the ways it had set me up for my career and the ways it had sorely failed. The Hendon training programme had been abolished and replaced with a new recruit programme called PEQF (Police Education Qualifications Framework). The programme formally recognized policing as a profession and provided the opportunity to earn while you learn. There were three pathways: one undergraduate course, which was the apprenticeship, and two postgraduate courses, which included a direct entry detectives route as well as general policing. This was essentially police training outsourced by the Met to an external organization. These university courses were written by ex-police officers and then approved by the Met, and it seemed it might be a great career path for me to pursue. Perhaps, given my experiences, people might not have understood why I wanted to work in policing at all. From the outside it might not have looked worth it. But I'd had a three-decade-long career doing a job I loved. I still had a passion for policing – it was all I had ever known – and I still thought it was possible to make a difference. Perhaps I could train officers to provide a better service to the public. I could instil that passion in young people at entry level and teach them about accountability, responsibility and ethics. Maybe after all these years it was from the outside that I could help change the toxic culture that prevailed in policing. I never managed to change it on the inside.

The PEQF programme was based on the National Police Curriculum. Each of these courses involved varying amounts of time spent on the job and then blocks of time released to a consortium of four London-based universities to study the theory. All three programmes were taught for the first seventeen weeks at universities by lecturers who came from the external organization to which the Met outsourced. All the lecturers were ex-police officers, so it felt like the perfect place to work.

I got in touch with them and expressed my interest, and after various conversations including a formal interview they said to me that they were interested in me joining, but not as a lecturer, as a team leader. They valued my skill and experience. There was just one catch: they needed to get the permission of the Met Police as they were funding the programme.

After that, I heard nothing. I kept phoning, asking whether there was any movement on the job, but I just kept getting excuses until eventually someone told me that I hadn't got the job.

'But I don't understand,' I said. 'You seemed so keen.'

Although I couldn't be sure, everything appeared to have changed once they went to the police to rubber-stamp my appointment. I asked if they were able to give me feedback about why I hadn't got the job, but I was told that the Met Police hadn't given any.

It was really soul-destroying. All I wanted to do was move on with my life, but, as my employment tribunal papers would reveal, the person they had asked to authorize my appointment was none other than the last chief superintendent I'd had, the same person I'd named in my employment tribunal.

In the meantime, I was approached about doing an interview with *Channel 4 News*. Journalist and presenter Cathy Newman had been in touch with my lawyer and she knew about the employment tribunal. Since before my departure from New Scotland Yard she had been asking me to sit down for an interview with her, but I was unsure. Perhaps there was still a part of me that didn't want to speak out against my former employer in such a public way, a part of me that was still loyal to the force I had dedicated my entire career to. But Cathy kept in touch. Speaking on TV was a daunting prospect. Each time I came close to doing the interview I would change my mind. In February 2021, a year after my departure from New Scotland Yard, I finally agreed to sit down and talk with her about my experiences within the Met. I had my voice and it was time to use it, however terrifying the thought.

Looking back now, it was too soon. Although I had left the Met a year before, I was still far too emotional about what had happened to me, the wounds far too raw.

When I watched the interview back I could see it written all over my face. I looked traumatized. It was then, seeing my blanched face on the screen, that it really hit home how much the Met had impacted me. I've never been able to bring myself to watch it again since.

The interview was broadcast on *Channel 4 News* and Cathy opened the piece to camera by talking about the *Macpherson Report*, which had found the Met to be institutionally racist more than twenty years earlier. She showed a clip of Commissioner Cressida Dick insisting that 'the label no longer applied'. That, of course, had not been my experience. In the interview, I told Cathy many stories which I have written here in these pages, about the racism I had experienced, how almost all of my opportunities to get promoted had been blocked in some way.

'Every day was just a battle, a battle to be treated fairly,' I told her. 'It was a battle at every rank.'

It was at that time I almost broke down. I knew it had been my right to get to those assessment centres, and yet it was true that by any means possible my path to them, my right to pursue a career path, had been blocked. I knew that, I had lived it, and I had seen my other BAME colleagues experience the same. Perhaps it was the act of telling a stranger and finally being heard that brought all the emotion to the forefront of my mind that day. After spending so long in an organization where the majority of people deny your experiences, you begin to believe it yourself.

Cathy asked me what had been the final straw for me.

'The last two years my working environment was becoming increasingly hostile,' I said.

I told her how I was afraid of what retaliatory action I

would face day to day, and my voice cracked again when I described how I loved my job. I stumbled, using the present tense, trying to explain that the blood of policing was still running through my veins despite everything that had happened.

'I'm proud to be . . .' I paused. 'I'm proud that I was a police officer, but that doesn't mean that I can be discriminated against, or the Equality Act breached . . .' I stopped, almost breaking down again.

She asked me what needed to change, and I told her that Cressida Dick needed to go.

'But it's more than just changing the player,' I added. 'It's about changing the game.'

Of course the Met refused to comment, saying that it would be 'inappropriate' ahead of my employment tribunal. They went on to give a statement that they do not tolerate discrimination and encourage all officers to report it. I thought back to the swastika on the wall and how I was commanded to keep my mouth shut. If only their statement had been the experience of me and my BAME colleagues.

It wasn't long after that interview that Zinnia pointed out a job advertisement that she thought I would be ideal for. It was at the University of East London (UEL), to teach the same postgraduate and undergraduate policing programme that was implemented by the company that had previously rejected me. The difference in this case was that the university itself was recruiting lecturers rather than the police.

I contacted them and was invited for an interview. I had a great feeling about it from the get go. The UEL had one of the highest numbers of ethnic minority students in the country, because they came from the local area. This diversity was reflected in the teaching staff too. The university actively wanted staff that looked like the cohorts they would be teaching – on joining I would be the seventh out of eight lecturers on the police programme who were black, Asian or minority ethnic. The university was not afraid of activist teachers who wanted to be a force for positive change and wanted to instil in their students critical thinking that they could apply to their policing work; in fact they actively encouraged it. Their approach couldn't have sounded more perfect. I liked what the university stood for and the fact that they weren't afraid to stand up to the Met.

I was absolutely thrilled a few weeks later when I was offered the job. I danced around the living room. Mum sat in her green recliner chair just watching me. If only she had understood, she would have been so proud. In fact, she would have danced with me.

The external company who implemented the training programmes raised concerns with the university, asking why they were recruiting staff who were anti-police. Of course they didn't name any names but I had an idea of who they were alluding to. That description didn't fit me anyway. I was anti-racism, I was anti-sexism, I was anti-homophobia, I was anti-corruption, but I was never ever anti-police. The company, on behalf of the Met, continued trying to put pressure on the university to remove us from the PEQF programme. But the university defended their lecturers and stood their ground, knowing that the future of policing was too important and needed the right people to teach and bring change for the benefit of all. For the first time I could feel proud that I was being backed by my organization. It was a feeling I wasn't used to.

The syllabus for the courses had been put together by ex-police officers with the oversight and approval of the Met's subject matter experts, and so for the most part they were controlling what the students would learn and who would teach it. I was happy to teach it however. The only thing I wanted to teach my students in addition was to *think* about policing, to consider the issues of the day, to consider the people they were policing and to consider accountability and responsibility. I could still deliver the syllabus and meet the aims and objectives of the course but in a way that would hopefully produce a new generation of police officers who were able to think critically, not just go along with the old status quo. The university welcomed this kind of teaching, and I was thrilled to have the opportunity finally to enact change. I was overwhelmed by excitement and possibility. At last, a new start with an institution that actually wanted me for who I was.

I felt re-energized, reinvigorated and hopeful as I commenced my job at the university. But just as things started to take a turn for the better in my professional life, things took a devastating turn at home.

Mum died in June 2021. In the weeks before she passed away I had been working from my laptop from the hospital, sleeping at night on a put-up bed beside hers. She had been my inspiration to keep fighting in the Met because she had never stopped fighting for a better life for us. She had come to Britain in search of it, and she had stayed here despite the odds, despite the hate. Her solution for racist neighbours was to treat them with kindness, to send me round with samosas, to win them over with love, not hate.

'Kill them with kindness,' she had told me. 'You've just got to work harder. Not everyone is going to like you, but you can turn it around.'

Mum had been my everything.

I went home from the hospital and sat in my living room alone. Opposite me was her green recliner armchair, the one she always sat in. Even if we weren't saying anything to one another she was happy just to sit and watch me, so strong was the bond we had, right up until those final breaths. She had been a part of my entire story and now I would need to write the ending alone.

The university programme ran throughout the calendar year rather than the academic one, with students spending some weeks in the classroom followed by weeks or months at their command units within the Met where they could put into practice all that they had learnt. The initial seventeen-week programme wasn't taught by the university's lecturers but by lecturers the Met had hand-selected from the external company. They would share the campus at the university with us for those seventeen weeks. As we sat in the canteen during that period, us university lecturers on one side of the room and the Met-selected lecturers on the other, it was like I was right back at Hendon. Once again I was confronted with an almost entirely white group. It was so blindingly obvious to see how the canteen culture that Macpherson had mentioned in his report two decades before had survived. They were all ex- or retired police officers, and they were all those same men I had encountered in the force. In contrast, our staff team represented something much more modern, much more reflective of the Met's supposed aims in terms of who they wanted to recruit as officers. Only this irony was clearly lost on the Met.

Police culture didn't fit into academia – it's just police training delivered at a university – but the Met still tried to extend their reach to the university. The student officers were instructed to dress smart-casual, and told not to interact with the other students. This denied some of them the full university experience, and I have to admit I felt a bit bad about that. But to my relief, the university took a firm stand against this.

The students doing the postgraduate courses would come back to the university every three months and do a six-, three- and two-week programme before going back into the work environment. With those students I might discuss what had been in the news about policing that week, what the latest IOPC report was about. I felt that the first step in moulding a compassionate and inclusive police force was to encourage a sense of self-awareness and accountability. It was important that they understood how the public viewed the force. Of all my students, the apprentice students were the most challenging. These were the ones who had been out on the ground for a year, and these were the ones who I found were most entrenched in their ideas about what policing was.

'Who puts handcuffs on people when they stop them?' I asked one day when discussing Stop and Search.

The whole class put their hands up.

'But are you allowed to do that?' I asked them. 'What does the College of Policing say about using handcuffs?'

They looked confused.

'But my sergeant says I have to handcuff them,' one person said finally.

'But what grounds have you got to handcuff them?' I asked.

'I'll get into trouble if I don't do what my sergeant says.'

I tried to impress on them that if there was a complaint, it wouldn't be the sergeant who was responsible, it would be them who had to answer to why they were not following policy. I tried again.

'So what grounds do you have to stop someone and immediately put them in handcuffs?'

Someone put their hand up at the back.

'Because they failed the attitude test,' he said.

'And what does that mean?' I asked.

Of course, I knew what 'the attitude test' was – an informal and unofficial risk assessment that police officers use among themselves. If they stop someone and they are completely compliant with their requests, if they say 'yes, officer . . . no, officer', then they've passed 'the attitude test'. But if that person instead asks them on what grounds they're being stopped, if they are difficult, or indignant, in response to being searched by a police officer, they have failed – and those young officers before me thought that was grounds for handcuffing them.

'Imagine the young black guy who has already been stopped for no reason three times that day,' I said.

'But I've got to do my quota of stop and searches—' someone said.

'Imagine he is just going to and from college, he's hard working, and on his way he's been stopped once in one street, once in another, and then on his way home he's stopped again. Do you think that guy might not be very happy that he is being constantly picked out for stop and search for no apparent reason?'

There was silence in the classroom. There wasn't a right answer that I was waiting for from them, I was just trying to get them to think about the way they were policing. I then continued with my lecture on stop and search policy.

'What I'm trying to tell you is that it will be on you. You'll have to justify why you did it.'

I wanted them to critically question and challenge. I wanted to see how the culture at work was affecting these recruits. Every time they went back to the Met for on-the-ground training they risked becoming entrenched in those old, toxic values. But the time they spent at university gave them the opportunity to think critically about their training and their actions and hopefully take some positive things back to their boroughs. I didn't want them to feel they had to accept things the way they were. I wanted them to feel free to challenge the status quo.

At the end of the class, one of the Asian students hung back to talk to me. He told me that he was being bullied at work, that he thought it was because of the colour of his skin. He didn't see the same treatment being meted out to his white colleagues. I sat down with him and went through his options. It was disheartening to see someone so young suffering through this. It made me realize just how young I was when I suffered the same, sent out to patrol alone in the dark.

That happened a lot. Students were too embarrassed and scared to talk about their experiences in front of the class in case it was reported back to their stations. They feared victimization. But there would be a queue of people waiting to speak to me at the end of a lesson.

On one occasion a female student came up to me at lunchtime and said that she felt there was sexism in her station. She said that the male police officers would insist on sitting outside clubs at closing time so they could look at the 'eye candy'. I was staggered to hear this was still happening. We needed to eradicate it. I offered her my support and we talked through how she could tackle it.

Another time a female officer, her father a high-ranking senior officer in a different force, told me that she was being harassed at work. Three of her male colleagues kept trying to talk to her about her sex life, and even followed her out of the station after her shift. They took photographs of her meeting a friend, and quizzed her the next day about who was in the pictures they'd taken. They were trying to intimidate and control a young female recruit.

Once, three girls came looking for me to share their experiences and seek advice and support. Their male colleagues were ranking them in terms of looks, placing bets on which one of them they would sleep with first.

I was horrified, and beyond concerned for the recruits. I didn't want anyone to go through what I had and I made sure to give them the support I was never offered. Perhaps I had thought as I progressed through the ranks that things had changed for probationers since I had been one myself, but if anything it had got worse. We see that in Baroness Casey's review, cases exactly like those I'm writing about here. But the only thing I and my colleagues could comfort ourselves with was the fact that while these students were attending our university they would never be alone in coping with this. We could put the right protections in place so that they didn't have to endure this type of discrimination or harassment. We had a duty of care to them which we were working our hardest to uphold, but where was the Met's duty of care to safeguard them? We had to report this to the Met and they had to take over dealing with it.

There are different systems in place now, but the toxic culture remains, and the Met still haven't learnt that words and initiatives don't create change – that can only happen from the roots upwards. The students I see in my classroom are the future of the force, so asking ex-police officers – the same ones who have benefited from a system that served them so well – to write the training for the PEQF is rather missing the point. The Met should be writing into their educational programmes different material and ways of teaching students to think critically about their work, to question and test the processes and procedures, to make sure the same mistakes are not made again. The Met did not want us discussing the Sarah Everard case with students and I questioned why, though no explanation was forthcoming. Why wouldn't they want students to learn from this? Why wouldn't they want the police officers of the future to understand how turning the other way from one officer's bad behaviour had damaged public trust irreparably, how it had cost one young woman her life? I didn't agree with the Met's censorship, so I did speak to my students about Sarah Everard. I even enlisted the support of Jamie Klingler from Reclaim These Streets (the group that wanted to hold a vigil for Sarah on Clapham Common) to speak to them about this blot on the Met's history.

It seemed to me that these young women and officers

of colour were still having to deal with the same old racism and sexism that I had experienced three decades before because of the Met's failure to deal with a culture that is alive and kicking. I had worked within the police service for long enough to see many positive changes in terms of streamlining and making it more efficient, but culturally it felt like it hadn't moved on at all. On the one hand it was depressing to hear these stories, but on the other I was so grateful I could mentor these students and help them to see that this wasn't normal. They had a right to complain, and I could explain to them how to do it. It seemed to me that these new students going into the force would be, quite literally, a force for change.

It won't be easy of course. Time and again I noticed that while the policing team did good work at the university, making these students think differently and sending them back for another stint in borough with new ideas, often by the time they returned to us it had all been undone by the attitudes of their peers, their superiors and the workload. They would come back soaked in that toxic culture. Some of the recruits clearly didn't want to be in the classroom, desperate to be earning their stripes on the streets, and they let us know this in the way they behaved. They'd sit with arms folded, openly criticizing the course content and being generally rude and dismissive to the lecturers. Sometimes it felt like I was standing in front of police officers with ten years of service under their belts, not new recruits. Some of the students would complain to the Met about the course and the Met would in turn complain to the university. I wondered how they would treat the public if this was how they acted in a classroom environment. Rather than getting too down about it, though, I saw it as a challenge. I had to change their mindset and get them to question their own behaviour. I knew that I was getting through to these students, that they would remember what I had taught them and how I had made them think. This was a chance to change things, to the benefit of officers and the public alike. That could only be a good thing.

I had hoped that my move out of the Met Police meant an end to controversy, or at least to my direct experience of the force's racism and sexism, but in July 2022 the company who ran the training programmes made news headlines for creating a case study for university staff to teach that was littered with racist tropes. The material had, of course, been written by ex-police officers, but when it arrived in our department it had been endorsed by the Met Police themselves.

The material featured a role-playing scenario that centred on a Turkish drug dealer using a Gurkha knife to murder a Chinese money-launderer. The case study had been sent out to all four London universities to teach, but I think that it was us at the UEL that protested the loudest. I don't know how it ended up in the newspapers – I certainly hadn't placed it there, although the Met tried to point the finger at me – but they were forced to withdraw it. It was just another reminder to me that the Met did not see racism because it did not concern them. If those case studies were written by ex-officers and approved by the Met itself, then they couldn't have been sensitive to what it meant to use racist tropes, or what the wider messaging of that would be to our students.

★

Nearly five years on from lodging my employment tribunal, at the end of 2022, things were finally brought to a close for both me and the Met by way of an out-of-court settlement. Commissioner Cressida Dick had resigned that April, and I had mixed feelings about this. I was happy of course, but also found myself disappointed that she would not be held accountable for the damage that had been done to the Met and, by extension, the communities of London under her tenure. Not to mention the damage done to my career, and that of other BAME colleagues.

In terms of the employment tribunal, the Met had stalled as long as they possibly could, perhaps hoping that the lengthy delays might persuade me to give up my case. It was as if they'd learnt nothing from my years of relentless refusal to accept their ways. Their investigations had found that there was no case to answer and the Met denied all my claims. They'd insisted that the employment tribunal would last for five or six weeks and the cost of that would be crippling, not only financially but mentally. I was certain it would be a gruelling fight, but after decades of doing just that I wasn't afraid of things getting ugly or listening to their lies.

The financial pressure, however, was more concerning. The Met were willing to settle, and family and friends encouraged me to accept it. At least that way I would be able to move on with my life without this hanging over me. I felt that the settlement gave me some kind of vindication and I finally felt free; the stress and anxiety that had been building finally diminished. I did, however, insist that I would not sign a non-disclosure agreement at any cost, and I was true to my word. After all, this wasn't about money for me. It was about standing up to an organization that was institutionally racist and corrupt. I was determined that the Met would not silence me because I knew that the only way to put an end to their deep-seated issues and the culture Baroness Casey had highlighted would be to keep bringing it into the light, to keep talking about my experiences and those of others. There is no price that can be put on my voice.

Mum had instilled this tenacity in me, but she also taught me to know when to walk away and fight another day. It's a sign of strength not weakness. Her words still echo in my head.

I experienced a lot of hate on social media and I still do for speaking out about the Met's cultural issues, from both serving and retired officers and their supporters, many of them using anonymous accounts on X. The canteen culture that Macpherson talked about had morphed into an online version – just as toxic but even harder to escape.

Those same keyboard warriors accused me of being a traitor and a hater, of being useless in my job, of getting over-promoted using my race. I had seen them call out other BAME officers who had left and spoken out about the same things. Their comments questioned why I didn't do anything about it while I was in the job. But what they didn't realize was that I was never silent. I had called it out from day one but my voice wasn't heard. I wasn't listened to; that's why I was forced to take it outside the organization. Because I believed that it could be better, that despite the bad apples in that orchard, most of the students that I was teaching at the UEL were the saplings that we were planting in the force – they would be the ones who would tackle the toxic culture, they would be the ones who saw through change. But would that be in time for the public to feel safe on the streets of London, or even in their own homes?

We know that trust is at an all-time low, we know that it is lowest among BAME communities. Commissioner Sir Mark Rowley admitted to being 'embarrassed and angry' at some of the stories that had been told within the Casey review, but to me his response was not dynamic enough, it was not what London deserved, and especially what female and black, Asian and minority ethnic Londoners deserved.

Sir Mark said on publication that the recommendations from the review would 'massively influence thinking and the plans we have ahead to reform the policing in London as we strengthen our work in neighbourhoods, as we improve the response to victims and as we tackle the toxic individuals in the organisation'. I have yet to see any action from these words, and that's what Londoners need to see if the Met are going to rebuild trust – action.

It is ironic perhaps that Baroness Casey had already addressed in her review this 'initiative-itis' of the force, claiming that 'Initiatives launched from the centre have insufficient traction by the time they reach the front line. Senior officers pull levers that do not shift anything outside New Scotland Yard.' What I saw from Sir Mark's statement on Baroness Casey's review was a lot of this lever pulling, but where is the real change?

'We found no shortage of initiatives to address culture change in the Met, but these generated more activity than action,' the review stated. It looked at some of the initiatives and discovered that almost £500,000 had been handed to consultancy firm Ernst and Young to carry out a 'culture audit' of just one department, Parliamentary and Diplomatic Protection. This is a huge amount of money to be spent on one arm that, for free, Baroness Casey found to be a breeding ground for 'some of the worst cultures, behaviour and practices'.

In February 2022, the commissioner sent an email to all staff with the title 'Enough is Enough', a new initiative for the force. In this email she said 'there is no room in the Met for discrimination or prejudice: racism, homophobia, sexism' and asked officers to 'leave now' if this applied to them. Somehow I doubt any resignations were forthcoming, and this initiative was dropped from all Met email signatures within a year.

But it is not for officers to volunteer themselves as racist, sexist or homophobic, it is for the force to root them out, and the way they can start is to listen to the people who are coming forward to tell them about these 'bad apples'.

Policing needs to accept that the profession attracts predators, who are drawn to the uniform and the power and access that gives them over people. To prevent another Carrick or Couzens they need to put a ring of steel around policing and not let these predators in. They need to have mechanisms in order to identify 'red flag' behaviour. That is precisely the bit that they are not good at, in my experience, in Baroness Casey's experience and in many other people's experience.

Ideally, police resources should be spent on policing the communities instead of on policing the police. We need to get back to community policing, people need to see those bobbies on the beat, they need to trust that they can approach them, that they will take their complaints and fears seriously. In short, the Met needs to go back to basics.

When I walk into my university classroom every day, I stare back at the eager faces who fill those seats in that room. These are the people who want to make a difference, and who will challenge and bring change. These are the people who want to join the force and wear their uniform with pride, just like I did all those years ago. Policing is recruiting brighter, talented people but they will not realize the benefits of this straight away. It will take many years to embed new values and practices, but with the right people teaching, it's all possible. The Met need to embrace these newcomers and the change they will bring.

I started my policing journey without accepting or acquiescing in the face of discrimination. I end my journey being known and being heard. My story is sadly not unique: it's the experience of many black and Asian colleagues in policing. I remained true to who I am and I'm proud of that to this day When I left the Metropolitan Police it was with my head held high, and now with courage I look to the next chapter in my life.

I still believe in the Metropolitan Police, despite everything that happened to me under its care. And if I can believe the police can be a force for good, I think the public can believe it too. I'm still committed to being a part of making that happen. My voice is my biggest weapon and I will continue to speak out for justice.

Acknowledgements

A heartfelt thanks to all who helped me in writing this book, and in particular:

To Anna Wharton, I couldn't have done this without you. Thank you for bearing with me. We shared some laughs and tears along the way.

To Robert Caskie, my literary agent, for supporting this book.

To my editor, Sharika Teelwah, for her editorial eye, care and friendship.

To Sally Wray, Louis Patel, Barbara Thompson, Holly McElroy, Rich Shailer and everyone at Transworld for welcoming and supporting this book.

To Lawrence Davies at Equal Justice for championing me when no one else did.

To the friends I've worked with over the years, Dr Nadia Habashi, Syed Hussain, Syed Shah, Shabnam Chaudhri, Amber, and Cherry Farley, for encouraging me to keep going and supporting my work.

To all my colleagues at the University of East London for believing in me.

To all the former Met officers whose stories are woven into mine.

Thanks to my baby sister Zinnia for teaching me patience and being that wise little voice in my ear. Thank you for challenging me, believing in me and putting up with me.

And lastly to my best friend Nina for being my strength and stay, for being there to catch me when I fall, for her unwavering faith and support.

About the Author

Nusrit Mehtab is a former police officer, at one point the most senior female Asian officer in the Metropolitan Police. In 2017 Mehtab instigated an employment tribunal against them for racism and misogyny, and soon after left the police force after thirty years of service. She is now a lecturer in criminology and criminal justice at the University of East London and also mentors many young recruits and BAME officers.

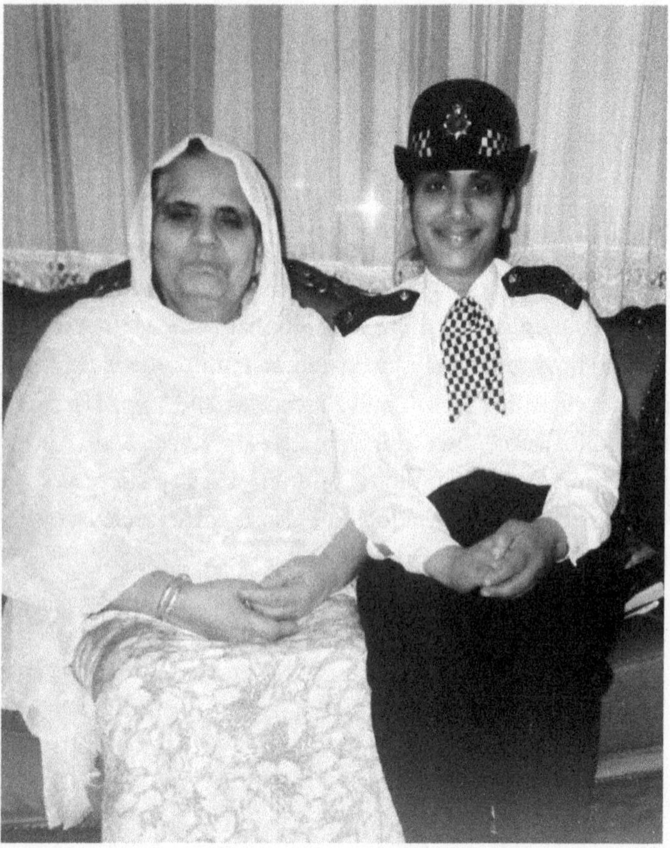